Graph Data Modeling
for NoSQL and SQL

Visualize Structure and Meaning

GW00776206

first edition

Thomas Frisendal

Published by:

2 Lindsley Road
Basking Ridge, NJ 07920 USA

https://www.TechnicsPub.com

Cover design by Manfred Christiansen
Edited by Lauren McCafferty

ISBN, print ed.   9781634621212
ISBN, Kindle ed.   9781634621229
ISBN, ePub ed.   9781634621236

First Printing 2016
Library of Congress Control Number: 2016948320

To my wife, Ellen-Margrethe, who fully supported me on this, my second book project. Being a writer herself, she was well aware of the implications!

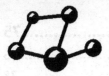

Table of Contents

Foreword: By Karen Lopez...1

Chapter 1: Introduction...3

  1.1. Motivation 3

  1.2. Audience 4

  1.3. Outline 4

  1.4. Acknowledgments 5

Chapter 2: Why Model? 7

  2.1. Model What? 7

  2.2. Providing Business Value from Big Data and NoSQL 9

  2.3. Data Modeling Heritage 14

    2.3.1. Evolution of Database...14

    2.3.2. Pointer Database (DBOMP) 18

    2.3.3. Hierarchical Workhorses..21

    2.3.4. Programmer as Navigator 23

    2.3.5. Chen, Entities, Attributes and Relationships 26

    2.3.6. Relational Model..29

    2.3.7. The Great Database War of the Eighties...35

    2.3.8. Objects Galore! 37

    2.3.9. Graph Models 38

    2.3.10. Object Role Model (ORM) and Fact Modeling................................45

    2.3.11. New Keys in the Models 48

    2.3.12. Data Modeling Conclusions 50

  2.4. Perception, Cognition and Psychology 54

    2.4.1. Perception and Cognition 54

    2.4.2. Concept Maps..58

    2.4.3. Conceptual Spaces 65

    2.4.4. Knowledge Graphs 67

    2.4.5. Cognitive Computing Example: Saffron 70

    2.4.6. Ubiquitous Pointer..71

    2.4.7. Think Spatially 72

Chapter 3: Real Requirements of Data Modeling 75

3.1. Post-relational Data Modeling 75
3.2. Finding Meaning and Structure 78
3.2.1. Working with Business People 78
3.2.2. Concept Models as Part of User Stories 80
3.2.3. Functional Dependency Profiling 84
3.2.4. Mining the Semantics 87
3.3. Visualization of Models 90
3.3.1. Functional Dependency Visualization 90
3.3.2. Understanding Structure and Content 92
3.3.3. Property Graphs 94
3.3.4. Progressive Visualization of Data Models 97
3.3.5. Tool Support for Property Graphs 102
3.3.5.1 White-boarding on Tablets 103
3.3.5.2 Diagramming tools 104
3.3.5.3 CmapTools 104
3.3.5.4 Graph database browsers 105
3.3.5.5 Graph visualization tools 108
3.4. Data Modeling Requirements 110
3.4.1. Solution Architecture 110
3.4.2. Business Concept Model Requirements 112
3.4.3. Solution Data Model Requirements 114
3.4.4. On Using Property Graphs 119
3.4.5. Physical Data Model Requirements 120
3.4.6. Keeping it Simple 122

Chapter 4: Data Modeling Described 125

4.1. SOLUTION MODELING (SOLUTION MODEL) 125
4.1.1. BUSINESS CONCEPT MODEL 125
4.1.2. POWER OF DEPENDENCIES 125
4.1.3. NAMES MATTER 137
4.1.4. FINDING PATTERNS 139
4.1.5. CARDINALITY AND OPTIONALITY 140
4.1.6. HOUSEKEEPING 142
4.1.7. MODELING THE SUBJECT AREA OVERVIEW 143
4.1.8. DATA TYPES 144
4.1.9. IDENTIFIERS, KEYS, AND POINTERS 145
4.1.10. KEYS 152

4.1.11. HANDLING TIME 155

4.1.12. DESIGN INVOLVES DECISIONS... 159

4.1.13. ABSTRACTION, SPECIALIZATION, AND GENERALIZATION........ 161

4.1.14. UNUSUAL CONCEPTS 164

4.2. TRANSFORM, OPTIMIZE, AND DEPLOY (PHYSICAL MODEL)........... 169

4.2.1. CREATING THE PHYSICAL MODELS 169

4.2.2. DENORMALIZE WITH A SMILE.. 172

4.2.3. KEY / VALUE TARGETS... 174

4.2.4. DOCUMENT STORES 176

4.2.5. RDF AND TRIPLESTORES... 177

4.2.6. PROPERTY GRAPHS 180

4.2.7. MULTIDIMENSIONAL MODELS.. 181

4.2.8. SQL TARGETS.. 182

Chapter 5: Selected Detailed Examples 185

5.1. FROM RELATIONAL MODEL TO PROPERTY GRAPH MODEL 185

5.2. A MULTIDIMENSIONAL MODEL 187

5.3. A SURVEY FORM.. 191

5.4. FIBO INDICES AND INDICATORS MODEL 194

Chapter 6: Before Your Expedition Begins 197

6.1. ESSENTIAL SKILLS AND INSIGHTS FOR YOUR "EXPEDITIONS"........................ 197

Literature... 203

Index 205

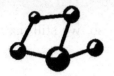

Foreword
By Karen Lopez

I started my data modeling and database career right out of university in the 1980s. This was around the time that data processing was undergoing a technological revolution: relational database systems (RDBMSs) were becoming increasingly present in enterprise environments. There was controversy, with Dr. Codd evaluating commercial products against his relational model, and vendors adding relational layers onto their pre-relational products.

It was both a confusing time and an exciting time to be entering the data profession.

At that time, data modeling was virtually unheard of in enterprise IT. When Information Engineering became popular in the late eighties and early nineties, data and process modeling were the *de facto* methods for designing database applications. Naturally, the logical data models for discussing business requirements used the same notation; it made sense to use a notation that mimicked relational tables. Entity Relationship Diagrams (ERDs) are still the most common method for expressing business and technical models. With the advent of data warehousing and business intelligence for read-focused database uses, we made some changes to data modeling methods, but these remained relational notations.

Fast forward all these decades and we in the data world are facing another revolution with Not-Only SQL (NoSQL) technologies. These solutions (often called "schemaless") came with promises of "no modeling required." Yet the IT world is figuring out that we still need logical and physical modeling. These models don't necessarily specify the structure of data, but they do describe the meaning and known features of data. We also have a perfect storm of open source projects, cloud technologies, and global collaboration. The result is more than a handful of candidate database solutions. In fact, we now have tens of thousands of database types, versions, and distributions to choose from. Even so, we still use tools and methods that express themselves in relational models.

In this book, Thomas Frisendal raises important questions about the continued usefulness of traditional data modeling notations and approaches:

- Are ERDs relevant to analytical data requirements?
- Are ERDs relevant in the new world of "big data"?
- Are ERDs still the best way to work with business users to understand their needs?
- Are Logical and Physical Data Models too closely coupled?
- Are we correct in using the same notations for communicating with business users and developers?
- Should we refine our existing notations and tools to meet these new needs, or should we start again from a blank page?
- What new notations and approaches will we need?
- How will we use those to build enterprise database systems?

Frisendal takes us through the history of data modeling, enterprise data models, and traditional modeling methods. He points out—quite contentiously—where he feels we have gone wrong and a few places where we got it right. He then maps out the psychology of meaning and context, while identifying important issues about where data modeling may or may not fit in business modeling. The main subject of this work is a proposal for a new exploration-driven modeling approach and new modeling notations for *business concept models, business solutions models,* and *physical data models,* with examples on how to leverage these for implementation into any target database or data store. These new notations are based on a property graph approach to modeling data.

I have a feeling we'll be seeing more of these proposals for helping data professionals navigate the data revolution we are experiencing. It's an exciting time.

Karen Lopez, Data Evangelist
Love Your Data, www.datamodel.com

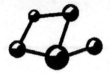

Chapter 1
Introduction

1.1. MOTIVATION

I have worked with databases since they were first commercially available on a large scale. Along the road we tried a number of approaches, some of which were not exactly right the first time (seen in hindsight). For example: data modeling left the business realm to become an engineering activity. The real world ended up consisting of improper table designs, surrogate (internal) keys, and other pragmatic solutions to real problems.

Then I discovered concept mapping: a form of concept model which today has been successfully adopted by the business rules community. I also followed the graph world quite closely, but it was the advent of the "property graph" style of graphing that triggered me to write this book. My intent is to set a new standard for visualization of data models based on the property graph approach.

One of the major differences between relational and non-relational modeling is the absence of schemas (in the form of pre-defined metadata) existing alongside the data. Once upon a time, names and data types were determined once and rarely changed over time. The new world, with its general lack of schemas or self-describing data, changes this. Despite the fact that "No" in "NoSQL" stands for "not only," most people associate it with "Not" SQL. In any case, the absence of schemas does not imply the absence of business requirements or the modeling of these requirements—a major theme of this book. We also will focus on the business requirements of good data modeling in schema-less contexts. Rather than modeling data architecture on complex mathematics, I believe we should focus on the psychology of the end user. If we do so, then engineering could be replaced with relevant business processes. In short, to achieve more logical and efficient results, we need to return to data modeling's roots.

1.2. AUDIENCE

This book is written for a few overlapping audiences:

- The experienced relational data modeler/developer who thinks, "There must be a better way of doing this." (And there is!)

- The people in analytics and data science who must prepare data for business and vice-versa, especially those in big data and advanced analytics.

- The developers who must develop data models as they go, whether they're in relational or non-relational tables, and whether they're on a traditional or new (like Graph databases) platform.

Most of the book is forward-looking and should appeal to many users, regardless of their level of previous engagement with traditional data modeling.

1.3. OUTLINE

This book proposes a new approach to data modeling—one that "turns the inside out." For years, relational modeling and normalization have been the name of the game. However, there's something upside-down in that approach, as we will see in this book.

To me, data analysis (modeling) is much like exploration, an expedition into the unknown. The data modeler wanders around searching for structure and content. The modeler combines perception and cognitive skills with intuition (which is a psychological phenomenon), to determine how well the landscape of business semantics is mapped. Mapping is what we do.

Two compelling events have made a paradigm shift in data modeling possible, and also necessary:

1. Advances in applied cognitive psychology have addressed the needs for proper contextual framework and for better communication in all settings, including data modeling.

2. Non-relational technologies (big data and NoSQL) have exploded in popularity.

Chapter 2 covers the background of data modeling. We will consider the roles of data modeling in big data and NoSQL solutions. We also explore relational and other widespread paradigms. We'll also highlight some concepts of human cognitive systems and our ways of dealing with our surroundings, including cognition and visualization.

Chapter 3 describes our understanding of the true requirements of data modeling. This chapter will outline the end user's actual spatial and conceptual needs. We'll end the chapter with a list of the real requirements of a data modeling solution.

Chapter 4 describes a data modeling solution that fulfills the requirements collected in chapter 3. We'll describe how property graphs can be used with concept maps to collect meaning and structure. Solution modeling for specific project data models is finally followed by transformation, optimization, and deployment for a number of different physical data store targets.

Chapter 5 walks through a few detailed examples. Chapter 6 concludes and helps you pack a "mental backpack" for your journey into the "data modeling zone," preparing you to explore business semantics.

The emphasis of the book is on solution data modeling (the "logical" level). Many of the new technologies are more or less proprietary, meaning that on the physical level we can only provide general directions in a book like this.

1.4. ACKNOWLEDGMENTS

Many of the diagrams for this book have been made in Omnigraffle (Mac OS X) and a stencil for property graphs that I developed.

Most of the concept maps have been made in CmapTools. The publisher of the software is the Florida Institute of Human and Machine Cognition (IHMC). The tool, which is free, can be downloaded from http://cmap.ihmc.us. It is easy to use and is ideally suited for brainstorming sessions.

Many thanks to Ilya Katsov, blogger at *The Highly Scalable Blog* (http://bit.ly/2adlkAS), who gave us permission to reuse his excellent "Stop following me…." illustration of NoSQL and SQL.

Marc Rettig created a complimentary poster on normalization for Database Programming & Design Magazine, published by Miller Freeman in 1989. The intellectual rights belong to Marc Rettig, now of Fit Associates. It is included here with his kind permission.

The EU-Rent Car Rental fictitious business is used in the Object Management Group (OMG) documentation for the Semantics for Business Rules and Vocabulary standard (SBVR), (http://bit.ly/2abzjp7). The EU-Rent case study was developed by Model Systems, Ltd., along with several other organizations of the Business Rules Group (www.businessrulegroup.com). The body of descriptions and examples may be freely used, providing its source is clearly acknowledged.

Some concept maps and text refer to my first book: *Design Thinking Business Analysis - Business Concept Mapping Applied*, Thomas Frisendal, © Springer, 2012, [5]. That book introduces business concept modeling, which is mentioned here as a recommended first phase of a data modeling flow.

My former colleague, Gopi Nathan, contributed part of a classic Bachman Data Structure Diagram originating in the late seventies. Thanks, Gopi.

Steve Hoberman, the publisher at Technics Publications and fellow data modeler, was kind enough to contribute some illustrations from his book [9] *Data Modeling for MongoDB*.

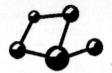

Chapter 2
Why Model?

2.1. MODEL WHAT?

In data modeling, you'll increasingly hear people recommending, "Start with the questions." The implicit claim here is that data modeling has historically not been business-oriented. Unfortunately, this is mostly true. This is a very important challenge, which it is now time to resolve, effectively. The focus must be on providing more business value, faster and adaptively.

There has been a strong desire in data modeling towards "building the enterprise data model." In my experience, very few organizations have succeeded. It is indeed a tough challenge, because business development is dynamic. Focus shifts, priorities change, product lines are terminated, companies merge, and so on.

If we struggle with getting data modeling sufficiently business-oriented, we probably should ask: Do we have the right framework for data modeling? The relational data model has been the model of choice for years. However, its name is not quite accurate and does not reflect what has been going on in real life. The most common approach has been logical modeling on the (normalized) table level using entity-relationship terminology.

This means that the transition to a physical model is a simple matter of transforming to the Structured Query Language (SQL) names and adding SQL technical constructs (such as constraints and indexes). Experienced practitioners will add views on top.

The logical and physical levels thus become too tightly coupled to each other, making changes more difficult than needed; and also dragging the "logical data model" away from the business-level. Because of the nature of the normalization process, databases became swarmed with little tables. Database structures with thousands of tables are now common.

In the early nineties, object-oriented approaches led to a great divide between objects (methods, inheritance, etc.) inside programs and plain SQL tables in databases. Object-oriented and relational developers started working on "object-relational mapping." Unfortunately, this method didn't work because the structural differences are in the way. Object-orientation is about classes, sub-classes, inheritance and so forth, and that is not necessarily the case of the classic normalized database. It helps, if the data model is designed within this context, but most legacy databases are not.

Additionally, many development frameworks (not necessarily object-oriented) introduced strict limitations on underlying data models. The data model became not only dependent on the physical DBMS, but also on the application framework model. Handling, for example, many-to-many relationships became quite difficult.

Sadly, in addition to the challenges mentioned above, the data model was rarely spelled out in the language of the business user. A few years after its conception, business modeling was either considered a one-page thing with some boxes and arrows, or considered the subject of the Enterprise Data Model teams' efforts.

This meant that we could not easily reuse the data models in analytical environments, which is a *de facto* requirement for all business-critical data today. How can we remedy this? By applying some data modeling skills.

The flow of a robust data modeling lifecycle looks like the model on the facing page.

The closed upper loop comprises the "business-facing" processes. From identification of concepts, to the creation of concept models, to solution data models—all of these steps eventually represent real business information. How fast you can accomplish one cycle of the business-facing loop is a measure of your "agility."

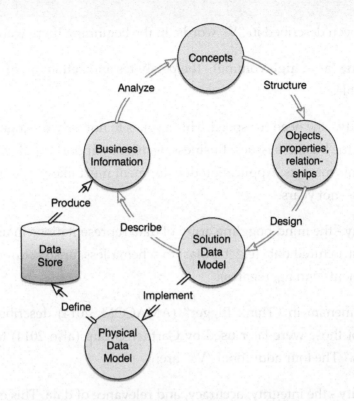

The black and gray shading of the arrows indicate various levels of rigidity and automation within the process: black arrows indicate high rigidity and automation (Implement, Define and Produce), while gray arrows indicate more flexibility and manual work. While there are ample tools to support solution and physical models, there's rarely enough support for the person doing the business analysis. This process could clearly be handled more intelligently, and now is the time to make that change. "Big Data" and NoSQL have substantial business drive and present some tough requirements for the field.

Let us look forward. How does this stack up to big data and NoSQL?

2.2. PROVIDING BUSINESS VALUE FROM BIG DATA AND NOSQL

At the end of the day, our goal is to provide value to businesses. When properly utilized, big data is more than capable of supporting that goal. So what's getting in the way?

Big data has been described in "V" words. In the beginning there were three:

- **Volume** (as in **high** volume) - the petabytes and zettabytes of data available.

- **Velocity** - the need for speed. This applies to not only the ingestion of data, but to the business issues. Business decisions support rapid changes in dynamic markets. Application development must likewise be completed in weeks—not years.

- **Variety** - the mind-boggling array of data representations in use today, from structured data (e.g. tabular) to schema-less, unstructured data (e.g. documents and aggregates).

Marc van Rijmenam in "Think Bigger" (AMACOM, 2014) described four more "Vs." Three of those were later used by Gartner Group (also 2014) to define "big data analytics." The four additional "Vs" are:

- **Veracity** - the integrity, accuracy, and relevance of data. This encompasses data quality and data governance.

- **Variability** - the meaning of the data. This is where understanding resides.

- **Visualization** - how the data is displayed. If you cannot see it, you cannot change it.

- **Value** - the ultimate goal. We must provide considerable business value.

All of these "Vs" pose real business development challenges. Some can be addressed with technology and others remedied by intelligent developers; most require a combination of the two.

From the perspective of non-physical data modeling, the relevance of the "Vs" can be evaluated on a radar chart, assessing the importance of each of the "Vs" on a scale from 0 (none) to 10 (very important). Following the radar chart is the reasoning behind each value of importance.

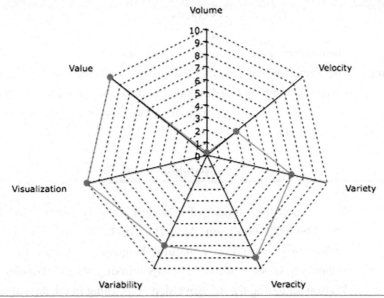

Chart by amcharts.com

Volume	
Importance	1
Definition	The amount of data in question.
Data modeling relevance	Volume relates to the physical data model, which should be designed to take advantage of the data store. Volume is mostly a technology issue (i.e. data storage efficiency).

Velocity	
Importance	3
Definition	The speed of data ingestion, as well as speed of delivering solutions to business problems.
Data modeling relevance	The ingestion speed is mostly related to the physical data model; it is mostly a technology issue (i.e. data store efficiency). Speed is also important for timely delivery of business solutions, which is why velocity scores 3.

Variety	
Importance	7
Definition	The many different types of representations of data.
Data modeling relevance	Variety concerns representational issues, which should not affect the business facing side. This is mostly a technology issue (i.e. data preparation), but also a concern for the data modeler.

Veracity	
Importance	9
Definition	The integrity, accuracy, and relevance of data.
Data modeling relevance	The three dimensions of veracity are meaning, structure, and content. Content veracity is mostly related to data quality, which is outside of scope here. From a modeling perspective, meaning and structure are of extremely high importance.

Variability	
Importance	10
Definition	Brian Hopkins, Principal Analyst at Forrester, in a blogpost (http://bit.ly/29X0csP) on May 13, 2011, defined variability as "the variability of meaning in natural language and how to use Big Data technology to solve them." He was thinking about technology like IBM's Watson for easing the interpretation of meaning in the data at hand.
Data modeling relevance	Variability of meaning is a show-stopper. It should be handled properly. In the Big Data space machine learning is being applied. Read more about this in subsequent chapters.

Visualization	
Importance	10
Definition	Graphical visualization of structure as an effective way of communicating complex contexts. This applies to both data visualization as well as visualization of metadata (data model in our context).
Data modeling relevance	Visualization of meaning and structure is the critical path to delivering real business value. You may develop a technically correct solution, but if your business users do not understand it, you will be left behind.

Value	
Importance	10
Definition	You must get a working and meaningful solution across to the business, just in time. In addition to value, there is also the question of relevance. How do I, as a human, determine whether information is relevant for me and what the implications are?
Data modeling relevance	Business value is the ultimate goal of any project.

Michael Bowers[1] has mapped the key issues of value and relevancy as shown here:

"Relevance for me" is subjective. As we try to make sense of a dataset, we look for a narrative that holds meaning for us. This narrative combines contextual information and relationships between elements into a body of meaningful knowledge.

Clearly, relevance and meaning are closely related. That puts relationships at the heart of understanding meaning.

Before 2000, databases were always described in some sort of schema. They contained names, data types, constraints, and sometimes also relationships. Many NoSQL technologies changed that.

"Schema on read" is a Big Data / NoSQL pitch that does carry some relevance. Schema on read refers to the ability to interpret data "on the fly." Based on the structures (such as aggregates or document layout) found in the incoming data, a schema-like representation can thus be built as data is collected. "Schema on read" is quite close to the physical database, and there is a need for another layer to do the semantics mapping. That layer was previously known as the logical data model and will continue to exist for many more years. One of the important take-aways of this book is that the logical data model is indispensable and the book offers guidance on how to go about specifying the logical level.

Quickly pinpointing the meaning and structure of data is more relevant than ever; more and more data will be available in analytical environments, where the data should speak for itself. However, this does not necessitate the creation of schema. In fact, it means that getting a thorough understanding of the business and potential value of the data is likely more important than having a detailed schema.

Dr. Barry Devlin, an information architecture veteran and originator of the term "Information Warehouse," recommends replacing the traditional schema with a

---

[1] Principal Information Architect at the LDS Church (The Church of Jesus Christ of Latter-day Saints) in a conference presentation from August 2015.

"Modern Meaning Model (M3)," which replaces metadata with Context Setting Information (CSI). Context is what information ingestion is all about.

Given all these observations, one of the essential questions of data modeling becomes: How can we gain a thorough understanding of data's business context—without spending months on modeling and creating schemas? After all, agility is key when it comes to delivering business solutions. This book will seek to answer this question.

2.3. DATA MODELING HERITAGE

2.3.1. EVOLUTION OF DATABASE

Before we understand where data is going, we first ought to be familiar with where it came from. Data modeling and databases evolved together, and their history dates back to the 1960's.

The database evolution happened in four "waves":

- The first wave consisted of network, hierarchical, inverted list, and (in the 1990's) object-oriented DBMSs; it took place from roughly 1960 to 1999.

- The relational wave introduced all of the SQL products (and a few non-SQL) and went into production for real around 1990 and began to lose users around 2008.

- The decision support wave introduced Online Analytical Processing (OLAP) and specialized DBMSs around 1990, and is still in full force today.

- The NoSQL wave includes big data, graphs, and much more; it began in 2008.

Some of the game-changing events (in bold typeface below) and first-mover products (in normal typeface) are listed here:

Decade	Year	Event
1960's	1960	IBM DBOMP (Database Organization and Maintenance Processor)
	1963	Charles Bachman Data Structure Diagram
	1964	GE IDS (Integrated Data Store)
	1966	CODASYL (Conference on Data Systems Languages) standard
	1968	IBM IMS (Information Management System)
1970's	1970	Dr. E. F. Codd: A Relational Model of Data for Large Shared Data Banks
	1973	Cullinane IDMS (Integrated Database Management System)
	1974	IBM System R prototype, First version of Ingres
	1975	ANSI-SPARC 3-Schema Architecture
	1976	Peter Chen Entity Relationship modeling
	1979	Oracle
1980's	1981	IDEF1 (ICAM Definition) - predecessor to IDEFX1 (US Air Force)
	1983	IBM DB2
	1984	Teradata (database appliance)
	1985	PC databases (for example dBASE, Clipper, FoxPro and many other)
	1986	Gemstone (object database)
	1988	Sybase, Microsoft, and Ashton-Tate port the Sybase relational DBMS to the OS/2 platform. Microsoft markets the new product as SQL Server and obtains exclusive rights on the Intel X86 platform
	1989	Kognitio (in memory database)
	The relational wave	
1990's	1990	RedBrick Warehouse (data warehouse database)
	1991	BerkeleyDB (key-value database)
	The decision support "wave"	
	1992	Essbase (multidimensional database)
	1996	UML (Unified Modeling Language) - object orientation
	1998	KDB (key/multi-value database)
	1999	W3C RDF (Resource Description Framework - semantics standard)
2000's	2001	Profium SIR (Semantic Information Router, RDF-based content management)
	2002	Aduna Sesame (RDF graph database)

Decade	Year	Event
	2003	MarkLogic (XML document and graph database)
	2005	Streambase (time-series database)
	2007	Neo4j (property graph database)
	The NoSQL wave	
	2008	Hive and Cassandra (developed by Facebook) go open source
	2009	Hadoop/Cloudera, MongoDB, and others
2010's	2010	HBase (column store, the Hadoop database)
	2013	Relational Hadoop (Cloudera and Splice Machine)
	2015	Apache Spark (in memory) and Apache Drill (schema-less SQL)

This table is based on many sources; the timeline represents the judgment of the author

The relational wave had some opponents:

- The (mainframe) DBMS vendors, who were late to join the SQL bandwagon, and were replaced by DB2 and Oracle
- The object-oriented DBMS, which never really gained a lot of territory
- Most recently, the NoSQL battlefield.

The data modeling scene has evolved in steps as well:

1. Bachman's data structure diagrams
2. Chen's entity-relationship modeling
3. Falkenberg's and Nijssens' object role modeling
4. A handful of variations on entity-attribute-relationship modeling styles
5. IDEFX1
6. UML and its class diagrams
7. Semantic networks and other graph approaches.

Today, boxes and "arrows" (crow's feet and many other styles) prevail, and much of the sophistication of the advanced modeling techniques goes unused. But graphs are making headway into very large applications such as Google's KnowledgeGraph.

We will take a look at most of the above, but before we get into that we present a little "phrasebook". For those of you who were not around in the 1970's and the 1980's, here is a small glossary of pre-relational terms:

Term	Explanation
BOM	Bill of material. The structure used in describing the parts of a product and their relationships. A multi-level parent/child structure that breaks the product down into components, or shows "where-used" relationships between shared components.
Broken chain	A disrupted chain of pointers, typically caused by a power failure in the middle of a transaction.
Co-location	A physical optimization technique where pieces of data which have strong relationships and similar volatility. Still used today in document databases and in aggregate designs.
Conceptual model	The business-facing data model.
Disk address	What it says: Unit, disk, track, block, relative offset within the block.
Entity	A business-level object.
Field	A data item containing information about a property of a type of record. Today called a "column" or an "attribute."
Hashing	Calculating a disk address based on a symbolic (business-level or "calculated") key.
Hierarchical database	A database organized in blocks, containing a tree of records, organized from top to bottom and left to right. Parent/child, master/detail, header/detail, and similar terms were used.
Inverted list database	A database based on indexing structures, some of which completely engulfed the data. The ideas are re-used today in materialized views, column data stores, and other NoSQL constructs.
Key	A business-level field being used for random access by way of indexing or hashing.
Logical data model	The data model describing a specific solution, independent of the physical database choice.
Network database	A database organized as sets of records connected by pointers.
Object	Originally referred to a business object. Later it was referred mostly

Term	Explanation
	to designed, technical objects in software.
OLAP	Online Analytical Processing. Became synonymous with multidimensional processing (early 1990's).
OLTP	Online Transaction Processing.
Physical data model	The data model to be implemented in a database of choice.
Pointer	A database "address" that points at another record in the database. Address was typically a logical page number and a page index, allowing for some level of reorganization on the physical disk tracks.
Random (direct) access	Accessing data based on either hashing a key, indexing a key, or using a pointer (as opposed to sequential access).
Record	A row in a table. There was no concept of Tables. Instead the term "Recordtype" was used, see below.
Record ID	A pointer to a specific record in the database.
Recordtype	The name of the collection of records describing Customers, for example. The same meaning is used today for "entity types".
Relationship	Introduced by Chen - before him the closest thing was "set" (in the network databases) or logical database (in IBM's hierarchical parlance).
Schema	A set of metadata describing the structure and content of a database.
Set	A collection of records, tied together by pointers (next, prior, and owner). A set had an owner and zero, one or more members (of another recordtype, typically).
Transaction	The same meaning as used today for ACID transactions (Atomic, Consistent, Isolated, Durable).

Let's have a look at some of the compelling events and first movers.

2.3.2. POINTER DATABASE (DBOMP)

One of the very first data stores was from IBM (in 1960). Its predecessor, which ran on magnetic tape, was called BOMP (Bill of Materials Processor). It was developed specifically for large manufacturers.

When BOMP was adapted for disk storage technology in 1960, its name changed to DBOMP (Database Organization and Maintenance Processor). DBOMP was one of the first disk-based data stores.

DBOMP was based on the concept of pointers: the exciting opportunity that came with the new technology of using rotating disks for data storage. However, developers soon strayed from raw disk addresses in favor of schemes with blocks of data and index-numbers. The blocks of data could then be moved around on the disk.

Here is a greatly simplified bill of materials structure (called a "tree") of a bicycle:

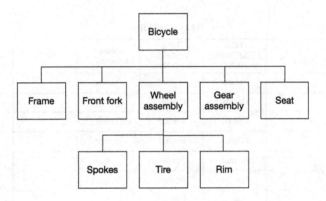

To read and manipulate bills of materials, a user needed to:

- Go from a product to the items used in that product, commonly seen as the "product structure tree." Wheel assemblies, for example, consist of spokes, tires, and rims.
- Go to an item's parent, or "where used," item. Front forks, for example, are parts of the bicycle.
- Advance to the next item in the structure; if the last thing you accessed was spokes, you'd advance to tires.
- Advance to the next item in the "where used" set of records. In the bill of materials above there is only one product; in reality, wheel assemblies could be used in mountain bikes, city bikes, electric bikes, and more.

- Return to the prior item (either within the structure or in the "where used" set of records). For example, if you just read seat, you'd return to gear assembly.
- Position yourself within the structure using a "PART-NUMBER" lookup, and from there you can choose to continue either downwards (exploring the bill-of-materials structure) or upwards (exploring the where used relationships).

As you can see, all of these actions rely on defined relationships, which at that time translated into pointers. Here is a simplified view of the basic DBOMP pointer structures:

ITEM-MASTER

PART-NUMBER	ITEM-STRUCTURE-NEXT	ITEM-WHERE-USED-NEXT	More pointers ...	DATA
	Pointer	Pointer	Pointer	
	Pointer	Pointer	Pointer	
XYZ-123	Pointer	Pointer	Pointer	
	Pointer	Pointer	Pointer	
	Pointer	Pointer	Pointer	
	Pointer	Pointer	Pointer	
	Pointer	Pointer	Pointer	

PROD-STRUCTURE

ITEM-STRUCTURE-OWNER	ITEM-STRUCTURE-NEXT	ITEM-WHERE-USED-OWNER	ITEM-WHERE-USED-NEXT	ITEM-WHERE-USED-PRIOR	DATA
Pointer	Pointer	Pointer	Pointer	Pointer	
Pointer	Pointer	Pointer	Pointer	Pointer	
Pointer	Pointer	Pointer	Pointer	Pointer	
Pointer	Pointer	Pointer	Pointer	Pointer	
Pointer	Pointer	Pointer	Pointer	Pointer	
Pointer	Pointer	Pointer	Pointer	Pointer	
Pointer	Pointer	Pointer	Pointer	Pointer	

Here is a more modern depiction of the data structure:

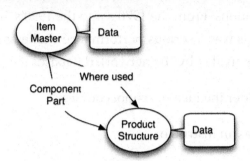

What you see here is called Property Graphs today, but we are looking at DBOMP in the 1960's. BOM handling is essentially graph traversal, which is standard functionality in graph databases. In SQL databases, BOM handling requires recursive SQL; this is not a skill for the faint-hearted. Here is an example:

```
WITH BOM (LEVEL, MASTERITEM, ASSEMBLY, QUANTITY) AS
(SELECT 1, MASTERITEM.PARTNO, MASTERITEM.ASSEMBLY,
    MASTERITEM.QUANTITY
FROM PARTS MASTERITEM
WHERE MASTERITEM.PARTNO = '01'
UNION ALL
SELECT PARENT.LEVEL+1, CHILD.PARTNO, CHILD.ASSEMBLY,
    CHILD.QUANTITY
FROM BOM PARENT, PARTS CHILD
WHERE PARENT.ASSEMBLY = CHILD.PARTNO
AND PARENT.LEVEL < 2
)
SELECT PARTNO, LEVEL, ASSEMBLY, QUANTITY
FROM BOM;
```

The pointer-based disk addressing was used in later DBMS products, including IDMS and Total. Pointers at that time were largely physical; you risked serious data corruption in case of somebody pulling the power plug of the disk drive, for example. The pointer still lives on (in a more virtual manner) today in the many new graph DBMSs, which are part of the NoSQL wave.

2.3.3. HIERARCHICAL WORKHORSES

IBM's hierarchical database system IMS (Information Management System) and its little brother DL1 (Data Language 1) were for many years the workhorse DBMSs of many large corporations. From the 1970's into the 1990's, a case like a large bank with all its transactions was a serious performance challenge. IMS was considered the best bet, but it was rivaled by the network databases (compared below).

For an example, consider the idea of school courses:

- Each course has an instructor

- There may be 0, 1, or more students present at any given meeting session (or "instance") of a course

- There is probably just one room assigned to the course, but the room may vary over time.

In a hierarchical database, the data store would be optimized for read access to all data related to any given course instance. This would be achieved by the concept of "physical co-location," in which a database exists as a hierarchy of "segments." Segments are retrieved by way of their root segment:

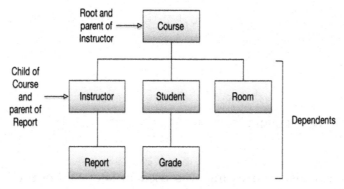

Based on information from IBM's Knowledge Center online

These six named segments are stored sequentially according to their place in the hierarchy: top to bottom, left to right. The parent-child relationships are top-down; there can be zero, one, or many parent-child relationships.

A course with all its students, the instructor, reports, grade, and room information would be stored in one physical block. (Today, this would be called an aggregate.) Access could be physical sequential (from the first course in the database and onwards), index sequential (based on a symbolic key, e.g. Course Number), or direct (using a kind of hashing mechanism).

Sometimes the model would need to span hierarchies. One of the ways to achieve this was "logical relationships," which spanned two hierarchies and appeared as new, logical hierarchies:

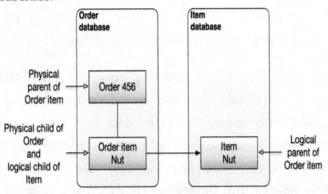

Based on information from IBM's Knowledge Center online

In many cases, IMS did a very good job indeed. It took years before DB2 gained similar levels of performance. On the negative side, IMS had a very complex and inflexible architecture that turned relatively small changes into large re-engineering projects.

2.3.4. PROGRAMMER AS NAVIGATOR

The 1973 Turing award lecture was given by Charles M. Bachman, the inventor of the first database system (1964). He described the new opportunities arising from the introduction of random access disk storage devices. The title of his talk was "The Programmer as Navigator." Primary data keys were used as the principal identifiers of data records, but secondary data keys were also employed.

Besides records and keys, Bachman chose the metaphor of the simple set for relationships between records. Not sets in the strict mathematical (algebraic) sense, but like "collections". To illustrate his point, Bachman presented a data model example with a department-employee set, consisting of sets of employees working in departments.

The physical model was based on "database keys," which were close to physical pointers. Relationships ("sets") would be navigated with forward (NEXT) as well as backward (PRIOR) and upward (OWNER) pointers, using the aforementioned database keys.

It's here that the notion of the programmer as navigator originated. Sets were navigated in all directions throughout their hierarchical relationships. The paradigm was called the "network database" at that time.

Consider, for example, employees and departments. A department would be identified with a primary data key such as "department number." Employees would be identified with another primary data key, say "employee number." Beyond this simple identification, we might need to identify relationships; this is where secondary data keys would come into play. Bachman actually invented the first kind of entity-relationship modeling. He called it a data structure diagram. The version below was (and still is) used with the IDMS database system, which appeared in the 1970's:

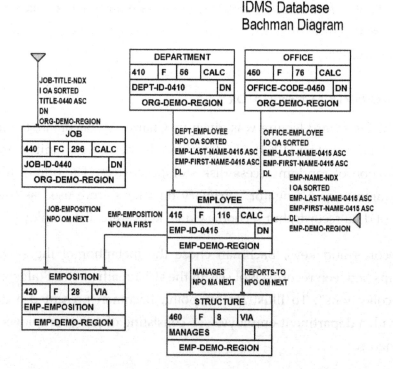

IDMS Database
Bachman Diagram

Bachman's data structure diagram was the first of many "boxes and arrows" diagrams. Most of the text annotations in the diagram are physical specifications for IDMS. Notice, however, that the relationships ("sets") are named.

The relationships were implemented as pointer-chains:

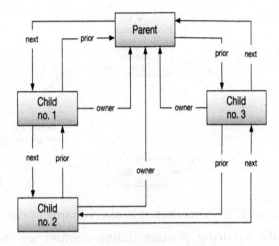

The pointers were present in a prefix to each record in the database, which was organized as pages with lines. Sets could be empty:

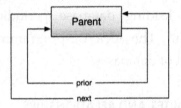

Or sets could have members as shown on the following page.

All of the links (called "sets") in the diagram are implemented as pointer chains (next, prior, and owner being the options).

IDMS quickly became the main rival of IBM's own hierarchical database management system (called DL1) and later the up-scale Information Management System (IMS).

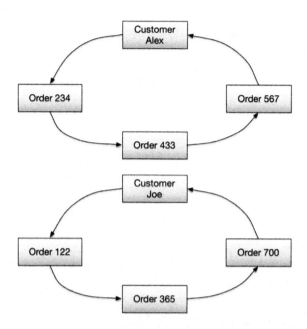

The major drawback of IDMS was that of broken chains in case of a power failure. That meant manually repairing pointer chains...sometimes in the middle of the night.

The network database context was clearly algorithmic: procedural programming. From 1987 to 1998, the leading database periodical was called "Database Programming and Design." The idea of programming was starting to gain traction, even in the context of databases.

2.3.5. CHEN, ENTITIES, ATTRIBUTES AND RELATIONSHIPS

The network database fit nicely with the entity-relationship data model that emerged around 1976. Peter Chen[2] was the paradigm's champion.

The diagram on the next page is a simplified Chen-style entity-relationship data model of our earlier departments-employees example.

---

[2] ACM Transactions on Database Systems, Volume 1 Issue 1, March 1976.

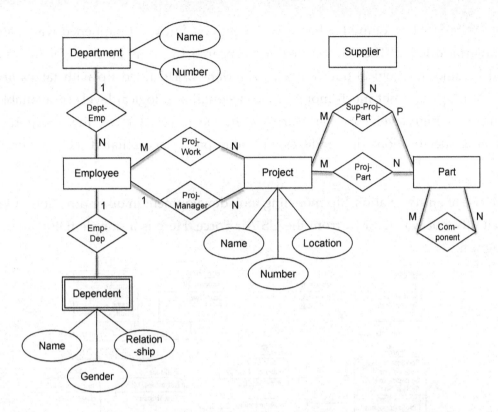

Notice that in the original Chen style, the attributes are somewhat independent. The relationships between entities and attributes are visible. Later on, in the relational model, they were called functional dependencies. Also, the relationships between entities are named, and carry cardinalities.

There is no doubt that Chen wanted the diagrams to be business-facing (i.e. what was then known as "conceptual").

In 1975 (one year before Chen published his paper), the ANSI-SPARC standards organization published its "3-Schema Architecture." In this architecture were three levels of models:

- External views

- Conceptual models

- Physical models.

The ANSI-SPARC committee had great intentions, but what happened was really counterproductive. The "conceptual" disappeared from the business-facing level and became the "logical data model." The data world filled up with tables and relationships and not much more. The conceptual and logical levels (if available) comprised high-level boxes and arrows. In the physical level, the addition of physical specifications (like indexes and tablespaces) necessitated the creation of physical models.

The rise of entity-relationship modeling took development in other directions. One such offshoot was IDEF1X from the US Air Force. Here is a sample IDEF1X-style diagram:

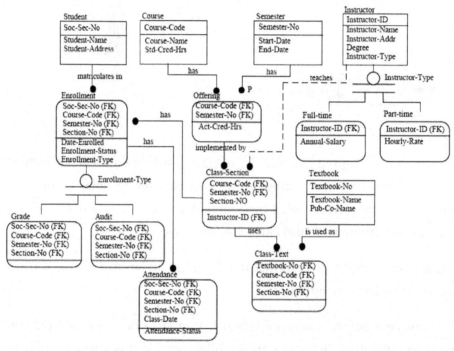

http://bit.ly/2ax3s01, by itl.nist.gov [Public domain], via Wikimedia Commons

The attributes were folded into the entities, which became tables. The diagrams began to fill with little icons, giving them a distinctly engineering flavor. At this point, conceptual models almost completely disappeared; most analyses started at the "logical" data model level. For instance, the following "logical data model" was inspired by a Microsoft MCSE training package from 2001:

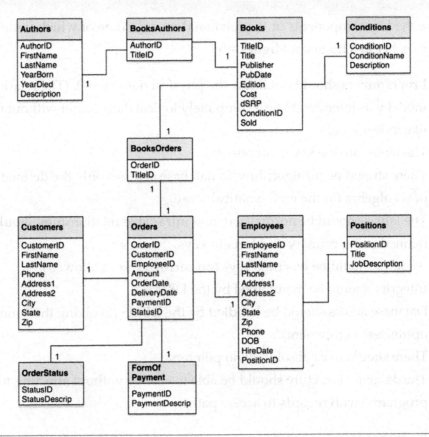

See the original "Pubs" database diagram at http://bit.ly/2ax3KUB

With the advent of SQL, relationships were no longer named or shown. To this day, I'm not sure why relationships became second class citizens. From a business semantics point of view, this was a very sad loss of information.

2.3.6. RELATIONAL MODEL

In 1970, the "Relational Model" was published by Dr. Ted Codd[3]. The relational model started as mathematical theory. It evolved into a full-blown conceptual framework for what was perceived as a forward-looking data model. During the late 1970's and much of the 1980's, Dr. Codd toured the world giving seminars on his model.

---

[3] A relational model for large shared data banks, Comm. of the ACM 13, 6, June 1970.

Here are the key components of the relational model, some of which undoubtedly helped to usher in a huge paradigm shift:

- Programmers should not know the physical data model. (The relational model was intended to be a completely logical data model without notions like indexes, etc.)
- The tables are the key components.
- There should be no algorithms in database access—only the defined ways of set algebra (in the mathematical sense).
- The tables should be normalized, and intra-table relationships should be defined using primary and foreign keys.
- All keys should be business keys (no surrogate keys allowed).
- Integrity should be maintained by the DBMS.
- Database access should be handled by the DBMS (evolving the "query optimizer" component).
- There should exist absolutely no pointers!
- The database structure should be able to change without affecting the programs (with regards to access paths).

The SQL language (Structured query Language) came out of IBM's database research labs in the mid 1970's. Before long, SQL was layered on top of several relational implementations.

This ultimately unhealthy marriage of SQL and relational models caused considerable confusion in terminology.

- A SQL table is not a relation (in the mathematical sense). Nor is it a relation variable ("relvar"), because relvars are predicates.
- A tuple is not a row in an SQL table, but a proposition.
- An attribute is not a column, but part of the heading of the tuple.
- SQL tables are not general-purpose abstractions to be used in all application areas.

The term "relvar" was introduced in 1995 by Chris Date and Hugh Darwen to create more precision in the discussion. The problem was (and remains) that "relation" refers to a construct of a named collection of attributes. In other words, it's a metadata object. A given instance of a relation is a "variable" (or name) that implements that relation within a given set of data. The proposed abbreviation of "relvar" was too abstract for most people, and it never caught on. Instead the term "entity type" prevailed, although it is not part of the relational paradigm. It's worth taking a new look at how relational data models can be designed. First, we'll consider the general approach developed by Chris Date; he formed the methodology of "normalization," which has been dominating the data modeling discussion for so many years.

The supplier-parts data model developed by Chris Date in his many books (e.g. [3]) has these three relvars:

SNO	SNAME	STATUS	CITY
S1	Smith	20	London
S2	Jones	30	Paris
S3	Blake	30	Paris
S4	Clark	20	London
S5	Adams	30	Athens

PNO	PNAME	COLOR	WEIGHT	CITY
P1	Nut	Red	12.0	London
P2	Bolt	Green	17.0	Paris
P3	Screw	Blue	17.0	Paris
P4	Screw	Red	14.0	London
P5	Can	Blue	12.0	Paris
P6	Cog	Red	19.0	London

SNO	PNO	QTY
S1	P1	300
S1	P2	200
S1	P3	400
S1	P4	200
S1	P5	100
S1	P6	100
S2	P1	300
S2	P2	400
S3	P2	200
S4	P2	200
S4	P4	300
S4	P5	400

The relvars are: S (supplier, upper-left table), P (parts, lower-left table) and SP (supplier/parts, the table to the right). In practice, "tables" are used much more often than "relvars," and tables have "rows" and "columns." However, "attributes" are also found in many textbooks.

In Chris Date's most recent book, he also uses the term "property." In discussing the detection of where attributes belong in relvars, he proposes that STATUS moves to the SP relvar (as detailed below). But he then continues: "Intuitively the wrong place for it, since status is a property of suppliers, not shipments."

Unfortunately, that opens up two new questions:

- If status is a property, why call it an attribute at all?
- From where is it concluded that status is related to suppliers? There are no indications of the dependency.

In Date's opinion, design theory is "largely about reducing redundancy." Nevertheless, he quotes Dr. Ted Codd for saying "...task of capturing...more of...the meaning of data is a never-ending one...small successes can bring understanding and order into the field of database design." I strongly agree with Dr. Ted Codd that capturing meaning is of utmost importance and that it leads to understanding and order.

The major lasting contribution of the relational model is the focus on functional dependencies, which lies at the very heart of data modeling. "Functional dependency" was originally a mathematical term indicating that something (a concept) is completely derived (by way of a function) from something that controls it (and possibly many other concepts). For example, a status attribute is describing something very specific, upon which it is "functionally dependent."

Let us revisit the STATUS column of the Supplier relvar, S. Is it describing the status of the supplier or of the city? What if it is depending functionally on CITY? Here is S:

SNO	SNAME	STATUS	CITY
S1	Smith	20	London
S2	Jones	30	Paris
S3	Blake	30	Paris
S4	Clark	20	London
S5	Adams	30	Athens

There is certainly some redundancy. We could eliminate it by splitting the Supplier relvar S into two, SNC and CT:

SNO	SNAME	CITY
S1	Smith	London
S2	Jones	Paris
S3	Blake	Paris
S4	Clark	London
S5	Adams	Athens

CITY	STATUS
London	20
Paris	30
Paris	30
London	20
Athens	30

SNC (the table to the left) establishes the relationship between supplier (SNO) and city (CITY), whereas CT (the table to the right) establishes the dependency between city and status. No information is lost in the process. The relationship between CITY in the two relvars is called an "equality dependency;" in SNC, CITY is a foreign key, which references CT. STATUS has found its home as an attribute completely dependent on CITY.

"Third normal form" is defined as the desired state. It simply means that all attributes are functionally dependent on the primary key of the relvar. STATUS is directly and only dependent on CITY above. Still, it is important to remember that third normal form (3NF) is not necessarily the best normal form. Here is the relvar SNP in 3NF:

SNO	SNAME	PNO	QTY
S1	Smith	P1	300
S1	Smith	P2	200
S1	Smith	P3	400
...	...	...	...
S2	Jones	P1	300
S2	Jones	P2	400
...	...	...	...

The relvar is in 3NF, but there are two sets of candidate keys: SNO+PNO and SNAME+PNO. QTY is functionally dependent on both of those keys. The remedy is to decompose (or "project") the relvar into two:

SNO	SNAME
S1	Smith
...	...
S2	Jones
...	...

SNO	PNO	QTY
S1	P1	300
S1	P2	200
S1	P3	400
...	...	...
S2	P1	300
S2	P2	400
...	...	...

SNAME was the trouble, but splitting the relvar into two solves the problem. The resulting model represents Boyce/Codd Normal Form (BCNF). Getting the keys and functional dependencies in order is the target of normalization.

Relational design also seeks to consider join dependencies. Date introduces the example of relvar SPJ:

SNO	PNO	JNO
S1	P1	J2
S1	P2	J1
S2	P1	J1
S1	P1	J1

The new attribute, JNO, stands for "job number," and the relvar represents a ternary relationship. It consists of three keys and nothing else, so there are no problems with dependencies.

That relvar (SPJ) is in BCNF, and it can be decomposed into the three basic relvars:

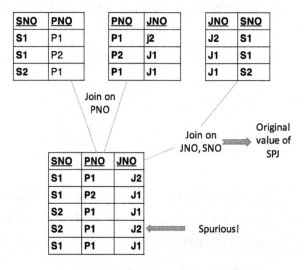

The join dependency of the third table eliminates inaccurate content (the spurious line); hence the so-called join dependency (and the decomposed tables) are not redundant. Another point of critique for the normalization approach is that it is "backwards," in that it starts with a body of data in an undefined state. Then it works its way through successive decomposition steps to arrive at the normalized relational data model.

Why this perspective? Well, it likely has much to do with the situation originally faced by data modelers:

- Forms on paper being manually entered into computers
- Sequential processing of punched cards or magnetic tape files
- Hierarchical data structures in IBM (and a few other's) DBMS offerings
- Network data structures in pointer-based DBMSs.

Back then, conceptual structures were only in their infancy and did not provide much help to the morass of IT programs filled with incomprehensible, abbreviated, short data names (many with a maximum of 8 characters!).

Another significant impact of normalization came from the realm of development frameworks. User interface classes dictated the structure of supported data models. Deviations from a hierarchical super-table / sub-table structure were hard to work around.

A major achievement of the standardized, relational database world was that of improved usability. Programming-free, end-user access blossomed because of the simplicity of the relational model itself, and later because of the graphical user interfaces. The relational model is a nice fit for general purpose reporting tools, but graphical user interfaces quickly became what everybody wanted on top.

Finally, it is fair to say that physical requirements have had significant impact on the data models that run enterprises today. Great strides have been made in hardware and associated technology.

2.3.7. THE GREAT DATABASE WAR OF THE EIGHTIES

Some argue that IBM prematurely commercialized its System R laboratory prototype into SQL/DS and then DB2. This is because Cullinet (IDMS), Software AG (Adabas), Applied Data Research (Datacom), and Cincom (TOTAL) had obtained high levels of account control in relation to the dwindling population of DL/1 and IMS accounts. Controlling the DBMS of a corporation was indeed an attractive position to be in.

However, Oracle was quick to build a commercial product, and within a few years, the migration from pre-relational to relational databases was unstoppable. A number of new vendors (like Ingres, Informix, and Digital) joined the bandwagon, but IBM got what it wanted. DB2 became the strategic DBMS for many large corporations. Around 1990, Oracle, Ingres, Informix, and DB2 matured into robust production DBMS offerings.

Thus database programming became focused on set algebra (except for stored procedures). No navigator was required—just a mathematician or logician. Tasks like recursive queries still posed challenges to algebra-focused programming, though. It took some 10 more years to really finesse; as recently as the early 2000's, people were writing procedural-stored procedures in languages such as PL/SQL (Oracle) and Transact SQL (MS SQL Server).

People have criticized SQL for being unstructured and incompatible with queries, and for being an incomplete language (in the mathematical sense). Given its issues, the question arose: if getting SQL was the ultimate goal, was it really worth the effort?

From a price/performance point of view, IMS and its contenders (the inverted list systems DATACOM and ADABAS, and network databases TOTAL and IDMS) were unbeatable. Their weaknesses were flexibility; physical database changes were difficult to accomplish. Almost everybody used SQL as an interface around 1990.

But the "real SQL" databases like DB2 and Oracle won out in the end. The replacement projects of legacy databases in IMS and IDMS started to take up too much of the IT department's valuable time.

By the way: the algebraic correctness of the relational model has been challenged recently. Algebraix Data's Professor Gary Sherman, supported by database veteran analyst Robin Bloor, claim that the structural problems dealt with in many of the classic relational examples are due to the fact that relational algebra is strictly not a proper algebra (because it is based on set theory, but it cannot be used on sets of sets). (See their free book The Algebra of Data, which can be downloaded from: http://www.algebraixdata.com/book/.)

Evidently, people slowly began to realize that one size rarely fits all. Many modern products have SQL interfaces, but some do not need them. New and ingenious ways of handling data stores by using key-value pairs and columnar structures have changed the data landscape. Add "schema-less" to the equation, and you have some really nice flexibility.

This is what growing up is all about: learning by doing. After some trial and error, we now know that relational models aren't enough.

2.3.8. OBJECTS GALORE!

A "resurgence" against the relational movement was attempted in the 1990's. Graphical user interfaces rose in popularity, and they required advanced programming environments. Functionality (like inheritance, subtyping, and instantiation) helped programmers combat the complexities of highly interactive user dialogs.

"Object Orientation" proved to be just such an environment, and it quickly became widely popular. Another advancement came from the Unified Modeling Language, (UML). They developed a new style of diagram called the "UML class diagram," as seen in this iteration of our department-employees example:

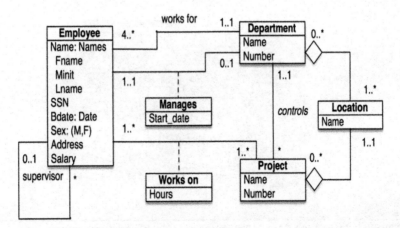

UML class diagrams focus on the logical level, and are declarative. But they are somewhat "stuck in the middle" between the business data model and the physical data model. The business data model should be business friendly; UML is not exactly that. Unfortunately, many so-called "conceptual models" (the model type name used for a product shown to the business people) are not intuitively easy to read.

And the physical model is still predominantly a relational, table-based model; normalized to the best extent that time permitted and budget allowed for, denormalized for performance, and only moderately digestible for business people. Object-to-relational mappings introduce additional complexity.

2.3.9. GRAPH MODELS

To make up for the deficiencies of UML class diagrams, graphs emerged as popular data models in the late 1990's. The development took three paths:

- Semantic web standards
- Document referencing in document databases
- Pure directed graph technology.

Note that graphs were not new concepts, even at that time. Graph theory has been a part of mathematics since 1736! The first paper was written by Leonhard Euler and addressed the military problem of the Seven Bridges of Königsberg:

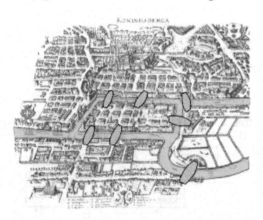

http://bit.ly/29VFWKh, by Bogdan Giușcă (Public domain (PD), based on the image

Aiming to solve an optimization problem, Euler designed a network of four nodes and seven edges. The nodes represent the "land masses" at the ends of the bridges, whereas the edges (the relationships) represent the bridges. Working with that particular representation is called "graph traversal" today.

Today formal graphs are an established and well-researched part of mathematics. In the data modeling community, however, graphs emerged considerably later. The graph types of particular interest to data modelers are "directed graphs." These are graphs where the relationships (called "edges") between nodes are directed. Directed graphs are part of mathematical graph theory. That a graph is directed means that the edges have orientation (from one node to the other). The directions are typically shown as arrowheads on the connecting line visualizing the edge. Directed graphs are a good fit for semantics and, consequently, with data models (which represent business semantics).

One of the great misconceptions of the data modeling community has been that relational databases are about relationships. They are not. In fact, the relational model focused on "relations" ("relvars") in the sense of having related attributes existing together, in the table representing a tangible or abstract entity (type). So the "relations" in the relational model are the functional dependencies between attributes and keys (which are also attributes). Traditional "relationships" (in the sense that there is a relationship between Customer and Order) are second-class citizens, labeled "constraints." Some constraints are supported by "foreign keys," which are as high as attributes can get (after primary keys, of course).

> The world is full of relationships, and they express vivid dynamics. This is the space that the graph data models explore. Structure (relationships) is of higher importance than contents (the list of properties), if your challenge is to look at a somewhat complex context and learn the business semantics from it. Visuals are a great help and visualizing structure is the same as saying "draw a graph of it."

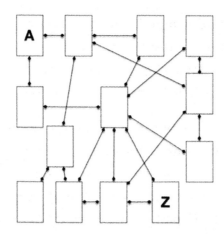

Consider the table relationships in the diagram above. Then consider writing the proper SQL joins for getting from A to Z. You wouldn't be able to, would you? The semantics are unclear.

In a graph database, traversal is much simpler. Neo4j has an example on their homepage (http://bit.ly/29QHLq9) based on the Microsoft Northwind demo database (see diagram and property graph in section 5.1). The database is about products, orders, employees and customers.

Within the context of the referenced Neo4j example above a business question could be:

Which Employee had the Highest Cross-Selling Count of Chocolate and Which Other Product?

The graph could look somewhat like this:

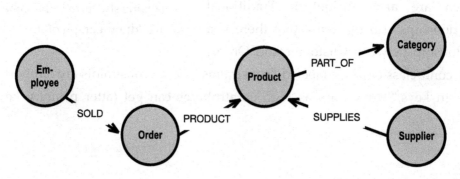

Formulated in Neo4j's query language, Cypher, the traversal looks like this:

```
MATCH (choc:Product {productName:'Chocolate'})<-[:PRODUCT]-
    (:Order)<-[:SOLD]-(employee),
    (employee)-[:SOLD]->(o2)-[:PRODUCT]->(other:Product)
RETURN employee.employeeID, other.productName, count(distinct o2)
    as count
ORDER BY count DESC
LIMIT 5;
```

(See more details at the Neo4j website referenced above.)

Notice how the path goes from product via order to employee to find the chocolate-selling employees, and then back via order to product to find those other products. "o2" is just a labeling of what we later want to count.

There are a number of good visual graph browsers available (e.g. Tom Sawyer, Linkurious, Keylines), with which you can perform traversals like the one above by pointing and clicking.

If you are dealing with highly connected data and want to be able to query it in many ways, consider a graph database solution.

Another interesting observation is that key-value stores and graph databases work quite well together. Nodes, relationships and properties are perfect candidates for key-value pairs. If the values relate to each other, you'll achieve graph connectedness at minimal storage cost in physical configurations. High levels of transaction support ("ACID") can be introduced, which has been the hallmark of relational DBMSs for decades.

The last ten years have seen the emergence of some quite successful commercial products. There are two primary paradigms, which are in use at more and more (and larger and larger) sites today:

- The "semantic web" category of graph databases, which involve networks of "triples" that represent subject-predicate-object "sentences".

- Property graphs, which extend the directed graph paradigm with the concept of properties located on nodes, and also potentially on relationships.

One of the great challenges posed by the internet is matching data. The tough problems revolve around business semantics. This space is referred to as "The Semantic Web" because much of the technology is based on standards developed by the World Wide Web Consortium (W3C)—the organization that also developed the specifications of HTTP, URIs, and the XML-family of standards.

Today the semantic web environment is based on the following standards, all of which are supported by robust technology:

- SKOS: Simple Knowledge Organization System. A system for management of vocabularies of concepts and relationships.
- OWL: Web Ontology Language. A system for management of ontologies (structured vocabularies based on logic) with inference possibilities.
- SPARQL: SPARQL Protocol and RDF Query Language. A query language for RDF databases.
- RDF and RDF Schema: Resource Description Framework. A definition and representation of concepts and relationships (the "data layer" of the semantic web).
- XML and XML Schema: Extensible Markup Language. This is the definitional platform for all of the above.

Precise definitions of the above are found at the website of the W3C consortium at www.w3c.org. All semantic web representations are expressed in XML. Schema facilities are available at different levels, but basic RDF data does not really require a strict schema in the classic sense.

OWL is by far the most feature-rich of the semantic web components. However, ontologies based on OWL are just as time-consuming to develop as UML (at a slightly lower level of complexity) and ORM/SBVR. However, OWL is very powerful; it performs well as a component of complex solutions with sophisticated requirements for the precision (quality) of search results.

SKOS is the "lightweight" component for the definition of controlled vocabularies. It is based on the notion of concepts and their relationships (quite similar to concept maps). We will focus on RDF in the following example.

Here are some facts about Woody Allen and some of his films:

- Woody Allen wrote *To Rome With Love*
- Woody Allen wrote *Midnight in Paris*
- Woody Allen wrote *You Will Meet a Tall Dark Stranger*
- Woody Allen wrote many more
- Woody Allen acted in *To Rome With Love*
- Woody Allen acted in *Scoop*
- Woody Allen acted in *Anything Else*
- Woody Allen acted in many more
- Woody Allen produced *What's Up, Tiger Lilly?*

Consider RDF to be the "data layer" of the semantic web. RDF is based on the notion of triples, as illustrated below:

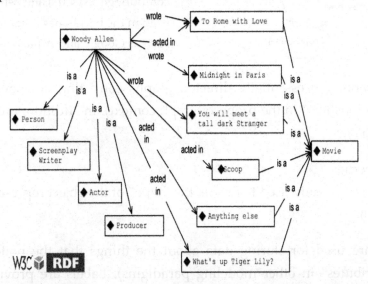

RDF "Graph" (simplified) of Movies related to Woody Allen

Each triple consists of a "subject," a "predicate," and an "object." For example, take the triple Woody Allen (subject) wrote (predicate) Midnight in Paris (object). Each triple may be read as a simple sentence.

RDF may be stored in specialized databases, of which there are plenty ("RDF stores," "Graph databases," and more), or RDF may be provided as an interface to a database (either as part of a database product or as a "bridge" to a database product). SPARQL is the query language (quite technical) that comes with RDF.

The property graph model is a relatively late newcomer to RDF, based on these concepts:

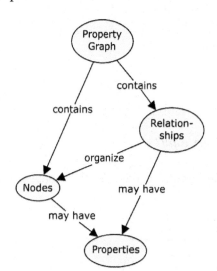

For some reason there has been a Berlin-style wall between mainstream IT and the RDF community. The latter is a community of their own and have been branding themselves as "Knowledge Management" and "Information Scientists." With the turmoil in the data store markets these last few years, this is changing rapidly. Semantic technologies are now happily married to cognitive computing ("AI 4.0") and semantics are used in the backbones of large companies such as Google and Amazon.

Property graphs are essentially directed graphs consisting of nodes and edges (called "relationships" in the property graph context). In addition, property graph nodes may have:

- Properties
- Labels (typically used to denote the "type" of the object represented by the node).

Properties are used for storing data about the things that the nodes represent (called "attributes" in other modeling paradigms). Labels are provided for just that—labeling—in some systems (e.g. Neo4j). You would use "labels" to denote that one particular node represents a customer, whereas another node might represent a product.

Relationships are basically connections, but they can also carry names and other properties. Properties of relationships are recommended to be properties of the relationship itself, such as weights, distances, strengths, or time intervals. An example could be ownership percentages between some property owners, and the properties of which they individually own some parts.

There are a variety of property graph vendors. One of the most widely used products is Neo4j, which uses this example to explain the various possibilities for building representations of real-world situations:

Labeled Property Graph Data Model

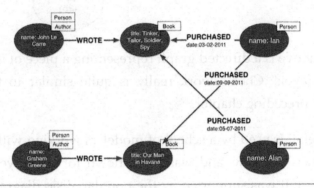

Source: **http://bit.ly/2ax29Ow**

The property graph data model is a simple, powerful, general-purpose data model. For those reasons, I recommend using it as a generic representation of any data model. As you will see later on, it is easy to map from a property graph to any of the popular data models used in the SQL and NoSQL communities of the world.

2.3.10. OBJECT ROLE MODEL (ORM) AND FACT MODELING

In his seminal work, "The Entity-Relationship Model - Toward a Unified View of Data," Peter Chen goes to the "binary level" before constructing his entity-relationship paradigm from bottom-level drawings, as follows:

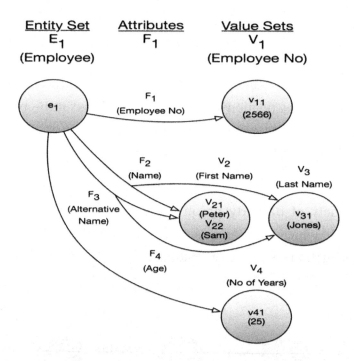

What you see above is a directed graph representing a piece of a data model at the most "atomic level." Chen's work really is quite similar to the graph models depicted in the preceding chapter.

This level of detail is used by a school of modelers working with "fact modeling." Their approach is not new, and was best known for many years as object role-modeling (ORM). It was supported by the popular Visio diagramming tool at the time that Microsoft bought the company behind Visio [7].

ORM is definitely at the right level of detail for data modelers (concepts and their relationships), but it also has all of the logic details required for formal, precise specifications.

I like ORM for many reasons. It is certainly more precise and detailed than the concept mapping discussed later in the book. ORM can handle even the most complex semantic challenges, and is adequate for describing business rules in general. However, precision comes at a cost. This makes ORM as complex as UML; consequently, it is not suited for business-facing specifications (the visual syntax looks too complex for most business people). Here is a very simple example of what today is called "fact modeling"[4]:

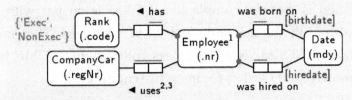

[1] **For each** Employee, birthdate < hiredate.
[2] **Each** Employee **who** has Rank 'NonExec' uses **at most one** CompanyCar.
[3] **Each** Employee **who** has Rank 'Exec' uses **some** CompanyCar.

One of the discussions that is not over yet, is how to draw a line in the sand between data models and business rules. First of all, business rules do fit into both the concept and data models. From an overall perspective, all those "if...then...else..." rules contain business concepts in the formulations of both the conditions and the consequences. Having said that there is still the issue about whether some specifications are at the data model level or at the business rule level. It is a continuous path with subtle transitions on the way. My recommendation is if it contains actual data in the text, then it is a business rule. For example, "... greater than 5 business days..." is a business rule, not a part of the data model.

Today, modelers of business rules use fact modeling. It serves as the platform for the new business rule standard called SBVR (Semantics Of Business Vocabulary And Business Rules). This standard came out in 2008, and the Object Management Group (OMG) defines its scope as such: "This specification defines the vocabulary and rules for documenting the semantics of business vocabularies, business facts, and business rules" (OMG 2008). Business rules are outside of the scope of this book. As a resource, I recommend the Business Rules Community: www.brcommunity.com. You will find there many

---

[4] Nijssen, G.M. and Halpin, T.A. Conceptual Schema and Relational Database Design – A fact oriented approach. Prentice Hall, 1989.

knowledgeable people working at the very difficult issue of business rules automation.

Another observation is that the complexity of ORM is on par with UML class diagrams, and also with the semantic web OWL standard. That makes sense, because fact modeling (ORM) is for business rules engines, UML is for object oriented programming, and OWL is for inference engines.

2.3.11. NEW KEYS IN THE MODELS

One of the assumptions in the simple variety of relational modeling is that primary keys (and by definition then also foreign keys) are single-valued. In many cases, though, this is not the case. Concatenated, complex keys are common on the business level.

Furthermore, even single-valued business-level primary keys can cause problems:

- Primary key values (e.g. employee number) may be reused by the business after a few years, causing trouble in historical data.

- Consolidation of data from different sources may lead to key clashes.

- The same physical object instance (e.g. department) may change its key (department number) for any number of reasons (e.g. organizational changes).

The notion of the "surrogate key" evolved to address those issues. Keys were first mentioned in the article "Relations and Entities"[5] in 1976. The idea is that the business level key is mapped to a system-generated, unique, surrogate key (typically a complete non-information-bearing number). This is considered by many the best practice in relational design today. There are also some terminology issues here. "Key" is not part of the business terminology, except for a few specific business subject areas. "Primary" and "foreign" are not familiar in the business

---

[5] Modelling in Database Management Systems, G.M. Nijssen, ed., North Holland, 1976.

context, either. What happens is that terms like "ID," "identifier," and good old "number" are used instead.

As for the uniqueness aspects, data modelers have adapted the very appropriate term "alternate key," typically denoting the business-level (singe- or multi-valued) key(s). The term is internal to the model and is not business-facing.

So what you end up is typically something like:

- A physical primary key as a surrogate key (with uniqueness controlled by DBMS-level features)
- A business-level "identification"
- A business-level "name"
- The business-level (alternate) key fields with support from a DBMS-level features.

Let us look at a subset of the department-employee example in this context:

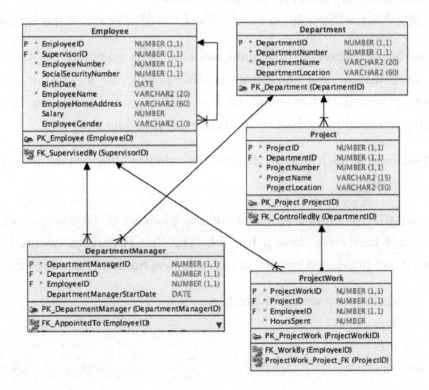

The system-maintained physical primary keys are called "ID" in this example. This is common, although I prefer the suffix "key." The business level "identifications" are EmployeeNumber, DepartmentNumber, and ProjectNumber. The absence of business-level identifications on the "many-to-many" entity types is questionable. It could be argued that introducing, for example, a "Project Work Registration No." would clarify matters.

2.3.12. DATA MODELING CONCLUSIONS

If we summarize the data model progress in terms of the Turing Awards related to data modeling, we get this picture:

- 1973: Charles Bachman with "The Programmer as Navigator"
- 1981: E. F. (Ted) Codd with "Relational Database: A Practical Foundation for Productivity"
- 2001: Ole-Johan Dahl and Kristen Nygaard for ideas fundamental to the emergence of object-oriented programming
- 2014: Michael Stonebraker with "The Land Sharkx are on the Squawk Box."

In hindsight, it is observed that data modeling was invented "on the fly." The results were diverse and sometimes counter-productive to one another. Now, however, pragmatism has come to the rescue; there seems to be a great opportunity to solidify the best methods of modeling data.

Let us look back at the history of database in a slightly different manner, as shown on the facing page.

There was a lot of ground to cover for the pioneers of Database Management Systems, and they have done a fine job. The first twenty to twenty-five years introduced and fine-tuned important technological fundamentals such as:

- Physical disk space administration
- Pointers
- Records
- Indexes

- "Random access" schemes (later called "hashing")
- Physical data model schemes based on hashing
- Physical co-location of data having similar volatility or life-cycles
- Multi-user concurrent update
- ACID (Atomicity, Consistency, Isolation, Durability) principles of transaction integrity and consistency
- Two-phase commit
- Journaling, logging, and recovery
- Memory caching
- Fault tolerance
- Distributed systems
- DBMS hardware.

The Pioneers of the DBMS Trail

1989: Kognitio (in-memory database)
1986: Gemstone (object database)
1985: PC databases
1984: Teradata (database applicance)
1983: IBM DB2
1981: IDEF1 (ICAM Definition) – later to be IDEFIX1 (US Air Force)

1979: Oracle and Ingres
1975; ANSI-SPARK 3-Schema Architecture
1976: Peter Chen Entity Relationship Modeling
1974: IBM System R prototype
1973: Cullinane IDMS (Integrated Database Management System)
1970: Dr. Ted Codd: A Relational Model of Data for Large Shared Data Banks

1968: IBM IMS (Information Management System, hierarchical database)
1966: CODASYL (Conference on Data Systems Languages) standard for network databases
1964: General Electric IDS (Integrated Data Store)
1963: Charles Bachman Data Structure Diagram
1960: IBM DBOMP (Database Organization and Maintenance Processor)

1960_____1970 _____1980_____1990

The relational proponents were struggling in the 1980's, with two major issues:

- Complexity of data modeling ("normalization ...") and of SQL
- Performance.

Even in its heyday, there were quite a few analysts who were not 100% sold on the omnipotence of the relational model. Yes, there were some good intentions and some good ideas. However, even to this day some serious criticisms of the relational model persist:

- Recently a mathematical incompleteness claim has come from a company called Algebraix Data. They claim that the relational model as defined by Dr. Codd is not really a consistent model since it cannot support sets of sets.

- Other criticisms accused SQL of not being a "well-formed" and complete (in the mathematical sense) computer language.

What really turned relational DBMSs into reliable, performant, scalable production tools was the advent of robust query optimizers. In 1979, Patricia Selinger of the IBM research center in San Jose described the optimizer of the IBM System R (a relational prototype system). Optimizer technologies matured during the 1980's and established the "relational empire" around 1990, as shown on the facing page.

I have chosen 1990 as the start of the "relational empire" because by then, the cost-based query optimizers had reached sufficient sophistication to allow the RDBMS products to take over most of the database processing across most industries.

Not much new relational technology was published through the 1990's and early 2000's. In fact, entrepreneurs (in California, mostly) were busy developing alternatives to the relational approach. Quite a few of the new companies and products were focused on specialized niches such as documents, graphs, semantics, and high-volume applications.

Today, vendors unite under the NoSQL / Big Data brand. In one white paper, a non-relational vendor (MarkLogic) very succinctly complained of relational models: "Relational database vendors are still offering users a 1990's-era product using code written in the 1980's, designed to solve the data problems of the 1970's, with an idea that came around in the 1960's."

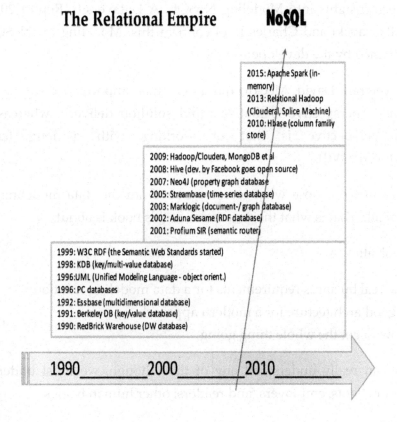

The Relational Empire   NoSQL

Around 2008, triggered by Facebook's open source versions of Hive and Cassandra, the NoSQL counter-revolution started. This space gets all of the attention today.

2008 was indeed a turning point. This can also be seen in the report of the very influential summit of database researchers, which have met in 1989, 1990, 1995, 1996, 1998, 2003, 2008 and 2013. In 2008, big data was the number one factor for a "sense of change" (The Claremont Report on Database Research, downloaded from http://bit.ly/2abBidh on 2016-02-27.)

So, where do we go now? How to balance the "what" and the "how" in light of NoSQL and all of the new technologies?

Well, the modern development platforms use schema-free or semi-structured approaches (also under the umbrella of NoSQL). "Model as you go" is a common theme, while data modelers and data governors are seen as relics from the past. Surveys (e.g. Insights into Modeling NoSQL, A Dataversity Report 2015, by Dr. Vladimir Bacvanski and Charles Roe) confirm this. Modeling for NoSQL is very often performed by the developer on the fly.

Database veteran David McGoveran notes this important distinction: the IT programmer's perspective is that of rapid solution delivery, whereas the data modeler's perspective is that of working with a long term asset (http://bit.ly/29PpWIJ).

How then can we choose what to carry over from the data modeling legacy, if anything at all? That is what the remainder of this book is about.

We will look at:

- The real business requirements for a data modeling solution
- A good architecture for a modern approach
- How to get the whole thing going.

Before we can really understand any of that, though, we must understand the nature of our clients, employers, and readers: other human beings.

2.4. PERCEPTION, COGNITION AND PSYCHOLOGY

2.4.1. PERCEPTION AND COGNITION

"Know your audience" has always been sound advice for communicators. As data analysts, our audience is primarily business-facing; even developers need to understand the business-level concepts. To deliver value to businesses, we must first understand how business people perceive and work with recognized information. For a better understanding of this, we turn to the realm of cognitive science.

Cognitive psychology comprises areas of research such as:

- Categorization
- Knowledge representation
- Language
- Memory
- Perception
- Thinking.

Data modeling is very much about communication of structure and meaning. Our target audiences are both business and IT professionals at many different skill levels. In perfect harmony with what is going on in other professional cultures (e.g. behavioral economy) we should also use the findings and recommendations of psychologists and cognitive scientists in adapting our ways to the human conditions.

I have been wondering for several years why we, the data modelers and system architects, create drawings resembling engineering blueprints when we try to communicate to our business-level clients? Try showing a UML class diagram to a C-level executive. Talk about communication breakdown.

To help analysts and business clients speak a common language, we can turn to cognitive science. A number of paradigms have been proven by research to work effectively for better communication.

Concepts matter

Psychologists who specialize in learning and teaching have developed a technique called "concept mapping," which is used in both elementary and higher levels of education with very good results. Concept maps are visual structures, which are easy to communicate. Consequently, they are a good platform for sharing user stories, which help us determine the requirements of the business.

Cognition is spatial

There are strong indications that our perception and recall capabilities are derived from our innate ability to visually process our environment. In other words, spatial structures are what matter most to our brains. On one side, this pushes analysts in the direction of visualization. On the other, it suggests we work with multidimensional coordinates. You'll often hear the term "conceptual spaces" tossed around in this regard.

Semantics are important

Since approximately 2000, technologists (also called semantic web nerds) have worked with implementing semantic technologies. At the time of this writing, the field is blossoming with brand names that run their businesses on top of semantic technologies. If in doubt, read up on Google Knowledge Graph, and try it out for yourself.

Cognitive computing is here

Knowledge graphs and even more integrated solutions are now readily available from Silicon Valley and elsewhere. Check out a company called Saffron (saffrontech.com), and you will see what I mean.

Let me re-emphasize visualization. It is really a powerful thing. Visual perception works on approximations, which makes sense from an evolutionary standpoint; if you were in the jungle and noticed something that *might* be a tiger, well, *might* was good enough for you to run. In this way, our perceptive systems have been strengthened by millions of years of evolution and now work quite well—even on erroneous input.

Rinadeg Oedrr

Aoccdrnig to a rscarhee at Cigdmabre Uinervtisy, it deosn t mtetar in waht oredr the ltteers in a wrod are, the olny iprmoatnt tihng is taht the fnst and lsat ltteer be at the rghit pclae. The rset can be a taotl mses and you can sit11 raed it wouthit porbelm. Tihs is bcuseae the huamn mnid deos not raed ervey lteter by istlef, but the wrod as a wlohe."

The example above[6] highlights the way that memory supports the quick scanning of words in a document—not all letters are needed to derive meaning. Our brain can fill in the blanks on its own.

---

[6] Interactive Data Visualization: Foundation, Techniques and Applications. Second Edition, by M.O. Ward, G. Grinstein, D.Keim, CRC Press 2015.

This brings us to the multidimensional aspect of data. The success of the multidimensional data model in business intelligence and analytics is overwhelming. Thinking dimensionally seems to come quite naturally to us.

This is probably because dimensional thinking is very similar to spatial cognition. At the "junction" of several dimensions, you find the information you need. So, multidimensional solutions give natural answers to the key question of location: "Where is this?" In fact, a "location" in a context is nothing more than multidimensional coordinates. Spatial thinking is again working wonders.

Recent research indicates that the hippocampi organs in the brain play a crucial role in providing access to the navigable representation of the both sensory experiences and conceptual constructs. The hippocampi are two finger-sized structures in the center of the brain (here in cross-section):

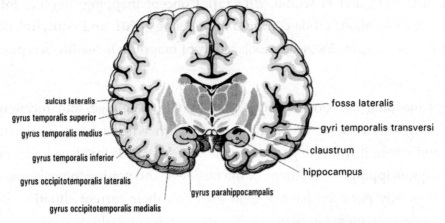

The cortex layers of the brain consist of billions of neurons. Our memory creation (and hence recognition) functions are based on reinstatement of paths between locations; the locations themselves are targets of different perceptions created by senses and reinstatement. Memories that last longer than, say, half a minute, strengthen connections between the relevant parts of the cortex and your hippocampi. Since the hippocampi have connections in many places, they are thought to play the role of the integrator. Having an IT mindset, this reminds me of some sort of a "hyper index."

Powerful communication can be achieved using the brain's physical senses. We rely on visual information for about 80% of our situational perception; clearly, using visualization in communication is a must. Brains are built, not least, for navigation. That is why structured representations in 3-dimensional space are generally the most effective visual tools.

This book presents an approach to data modeling based on these cognitive findings. Is it possible to do data modeling without tables and schemas? You bet. And it might just work more effectively, too.

2.4.2. CONCEPT MAPS

Concept mapping comes from the field of learning psychology, and has proven to be useful to both business experts and business analysts (Moon, Hoffman, Novak, Canas, 2011, [11], and Frisendal, 2013 [5]). Concept mapping involves intuitive, visual communication. While conceptual modeling (UML and entity-relationship diagrams) failed as business-side tools, concept mapping is readily accepted in its place.

Concept mapping traditionally deals with people, language, and meaning—not engineering. The issue of becoming familiar with what a business is currently doing and where it wants to go is a people-based issue. It involves brainstorming workshops, mapping the language of the business, and getting the meanings right. A business may not even have a good grasp on their current situation; concept mapping can help them figure out their starting point and ultimate goals.

Contrary to common wisdom, business analysis is not "just a documentation issue." It is a learning process both for the analyst and for the business itself. Concept mapping works in this context because it is based on psychology (the theory of meaningful learning), not on an engineering mindset.

Let us examine a simple example: The EU-Rent Car Rental.

The EU-Rent Car Rental is a fictitious business used in the OMG documentation for the Semantics for Business Rules and Vocabulary standard, SBVR, (http://bit.ly/2abzjp7).

The EU-Rent case study was developed by Model Systems, Ltd., along with several other organizations of the Business Rules Group (www.businessrulegroup.com), and has been used by many organizations. The body of descriptions and examples may be freely used, providing its source is clearly acknowledged.

The user story goes as follows:

> *EU-Rent rents cars to its customers. Customers may be individuals or companies. Different models of cars are offered, organized into groups. All cars in a group are charged at the same rate. A car may be rented by a booking made in advance or by a 'walk-in' customer on the day of rental. A rental booking specifies the car group required, the start and end dates/times of the rental and the EU-Rent branch from which the rental is to start. Optionally, the reservation may specify a one-way rental (in which the car is returned to a branch different from the pick-up branch) and may request a specific car model within the required group.*

> *EU-Rent has a loyalty club. Customers who join accumulate points that they can use to pay for rentals. EU-Rent from time to time offers discounts and free upgrades, subject to conditions.*

> *EU-Rent records 'bad experiences' with customers (such as unauthorized late return from rental, or damage to car during rental) and may refuse subsequent rental reservations from such customers.*

The text above is pretty clear and well written. However, experience has shown that representing the same information in a concept map will make it more intuitive to read and understand. The diagram below represents almost all of the information in the text above:

The concept map really speaks for itself, which is the whole idea. Notice that you can read little sentences like "customer issues booking" and "car group has a rate" just by following the flow of the map. Full sentences don't actually exist, but our brain has enough information to "fill in the blanks" thanks to the connecting lines between the concepts. Concept maps can be drawn easily in brainstorming workshops; they are easy to maintain and accessible for non-technical users.

Another key benefit to concept maps is that they rarely represent one-way narratives with a "start" and a "stop." Mapping a concept reveals a sort of "lifecycle" for the user's story.

You start by getting an overview of the whole story. The model on the facing page captures an overview of our car rental business.

From there, you must break down the objects shown on the overview, adding more detailed information. You may also "roll up" concepts and properties from forms and database descriptions, from the bottom up. You could, for example, look at a booking form and transfer the fields found on that to the concept map. Doing this adds more detail and in practice you work in a combination of top-down and bottom-up, depending on which information is available.

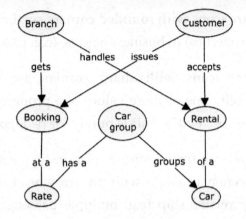

Here is a map of the information breakdown of the cars object:

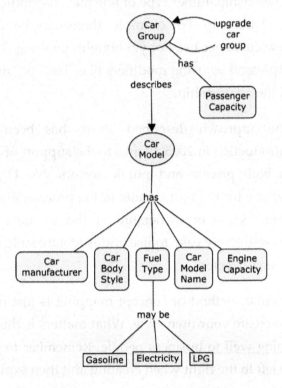

Here is a short description of the syntax used in detailed concept mapping:

Round icons symbolize business objects, which can include physical objects (e.g. goods), documents (e.g. invoices), players / agents (e.g. people, organizations), or events/transactions (e.g. sales, posting, distribution).

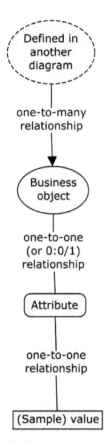

Square icons with rounded corners symbolize the characteristics (or properties) of business objects, (e.g. product weight).

Square icons with sharp corners are used occasionally to exemplify one or more values of a property (e.g. "British Racing Green" or "Red"). This is purely for pedagogical reasons.

Connecting lines indicate relationships between concepts. If the connection is made with an arrowhead, it indicates a one-to-many relationship (e.g. multiple passengers per trip). Without the arrowhead, the meaning is that there is either a 1-1 or a 0-1 relationship. Either type of line may also indicate that there is not a relationship. For example, there may be a situation where a new customer has not yet bought anything. These variations are expressed by using modifiers like "has" or "may" within the text of the relationship.

The approach described above has been refined since its introduction in 2005, thanks to the support of a number of clients in both private and public sectors. No IT or data modeling background is necessary for the participants in the process. Business stakeholders get a strong and real sense of ownership of the business information asset. Concept mapping is intuitively easy to use and is ideally suited for brainstorming sessions around a data projector.

However, this particular method of concept mapping is just one communication method. Feel free to create your own style. What matters is that the concept maps communicate meaning well to business people. Remember to work from the top down and from the left to right when creating and then explaining a diagram.

In addition to the concept maps, many analysts also capture and record (in Word or Excel) information about:

1. The verbal definitions of the concepts.
2. The necessary long-term business rules.

Verbal descriptions could be along these lines: "Concept: Car Movement. Definition: Planned movement of a rental car of a specified car group from a sending branch to a receiving branch."

Sometimes people mistake "mind maps" for concept maps. There are two major differences between a concept map and a mind map:

- The concept map is organized top-down (and possibly also left-to-right). The mind map has emphasis on a central concept in the middle of a hierarchical structure. Concept maps are directed graphs with restrictions on structure.

- In the concept map, there are concepts (in the boxes) and "linking phrases" (the named relationships between concepts). Most mind maps do not name the relationships in this way.

Concept maps were originally designed and developed by Professor Joseph Novak (Novak 1990, 2008) with a learning focus. The theory behind concept maps is based on Professor D. Ausubel's work on meaningful learning. This theory of meaningful learning suggests that learning is based on representational and combinatorial processes, which occur only when we receive information.

In other words, there are two processes: <u>Discovery</u> (of information) that leads to <u>reception of the information</u> (a.k.a. learning), integrated with what the learner already knows. In this manner, concept mapping is not only facilitating learning, but also creativity.

The key to successful concept mapping in the business setting, then, is to clearly depict the relationships between the basic concepts and terms used. Learning then takes place by assimilating new concepts into existing conceptual structures known to the learner. That is precisely what Professor Novak designed concept maps to do (Novak 2008).

The psychological aspects of concept mapping relate closely to those cognitive processes that help analysts better understand their clients and users. This is why I highly recommend using them for business-facing concept models. This is an area with some standardization:

- The International Institute of Business Analysis (IIBA) recently released <u>Business Analysis Body of Knowledge</u> (BABOK) version 3, which devotes a new section to concept models.

- A solid standard exists for concept models: OMG's <u>Semantics of Business Vocabulary and Business Rules</u> (SBVR).

Sometimes working with concept maps creates new insights (or "aha moments"). My book on business concept mapping [5] uses this concept map to outline the ideas of the book:

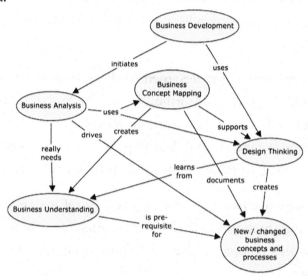

We won't get into much more detail about the analysis process, so I'll refer you to that book to learn more. It will be helpful if you are facing major analysis and design work having large and/or complex user stories.

The tool that I use for drawing the concept maps is called CmapTools. It is based on theoretical work done in the eighties and the nineties by Professor Joseph D. Novak. The tool as we know it today was developed around 2000; it picked up speed in the educational sector a couple of years later. Today, the publisher of the software is the Florida Institute of Human and Machine Cognition, IHMC.

The tool, which is free, can be downloaded from its website at http://cmap.ihmc.us. It is intuitively easy to use and is ideally suited for brainstorming sessions around a data projector. There are plenty of sources of guidance to CmapTools on the Internet, not least on IHMC's website: http://bit.ly/2aaZlI5.

2.4.3. CONCEPTUAL SPACES

We humans have strived to understand the structure of meaning for as long as speech has existed. Since data models essentially "speak" to their readers, we must consider the way we humans actually interpret meaning.

Advances in both neuroscience and cognitive science still point in many directions (because there are many issues), but there is a clear convergence toward a field called "Cognitive Spaces" (see, for example, The Geometry of Meaning - Semantics based on Conceptual Spaces, [6]).

A "meaning domain" consists of a set of values, which are points in a space; the space is structured according to categories, qualities, or dimensions. Think of spaces as a mathematical coordinate system (in reality with many more axes):

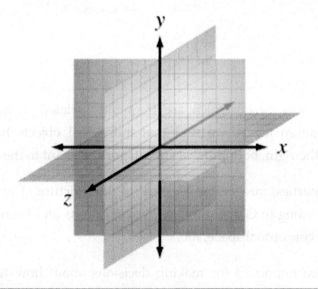

In this manner, there is a geometrical distance between objects; this is a more precise representation than the brute force "similarity" measured by machine learning algorithms, for example.

Note that there may exist both perceived qualities, which we handle psychologically (sensory data of color perception, for example), and abstract qualities subject to cultural variations.

Gärdenfors uses an example of skin colors within the complete spindle of colors used by visual designers. I created a simplified representation of a skin color subset of a conceptual space:

All colors

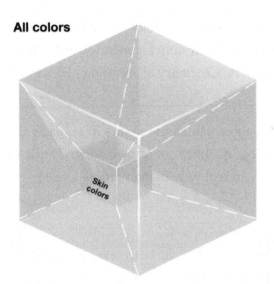

Skin colors

The bottom line is that we should think of objects of interest as residing in a multi-dimensional space. Our cognitive processes derive distance between points in that space, in order to arrive at categorizations such as, "If it looks like a duck, walks like a duck and talks like a duck, it is a duck!"

Objects come in categories, which are frequently related in quasi-hierarchical ways. At the bottom levels, we find that individual objects have coordinates placing them in the right, bottom-level subcategory relevant to the object.

Adjectives (properties) are certainly part of the picture. Categories (quality dimensions, according to Gärdenfors) also cover actions and events, meaning that verbs fit into the conceptual space, too.

These matters are important for making decisions about how to best represent data models. A network of directed objects (semantic graphs) is certainly a very intuitive way to represent semantic structures. Other technology paradigms (like the semantic web tools RDF and OWL) are quite powerful. However, they are not really *semantic* in the sense that cognitive scientists define semantics (as described above).

The field of conceptual spaces is certainly an important research area that strengthens concept-based modeling. Although conceptual spaces have evolved in academia over the last fifteen years, they still reside primarily there. However, they are increasingly being used in practice. There even exists an XML dialect called Conceptual Space Markup Language.

2.4.4. KNOWLEDGE GRAPHS

Google has introduced its new generation of web searching, called "knowledge graphs." These knowledge graphs deal with meaning. According to Google, "The words you use in formulating your search can often have more than one meaning. With the knowledge graph we can understand the difference, and help you narrow your results to find just the answers you're looking for." (See http://bit.ly/2bg5C5s.)

Here is an incarnation of the knowledge graph that appears if you search for people, companies, or many other types of entities:

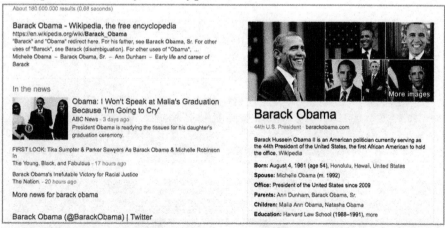

When you examine knowledge graph technology in more detail, you discover that a "knowledge graph" is essentially the same kind of structure as a concept map—

just supplemented with technical details. Here I have sketched a little concept map of the knowledge graph items that we found in our web search above:

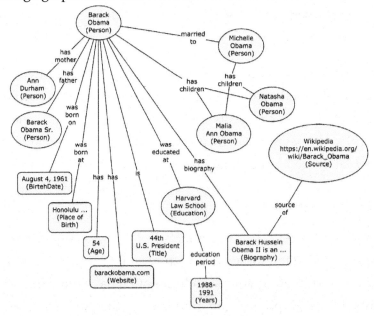

In the concept map above, I mixed both instances and metadata. This will help give you a picture of what knowledge graphs will look like in reality, from a pure metadata perspective. A knowledge graph is really a semantic network. Many semantic networks are based on the W3C (w3c.org) Semantic Web stack of tools:

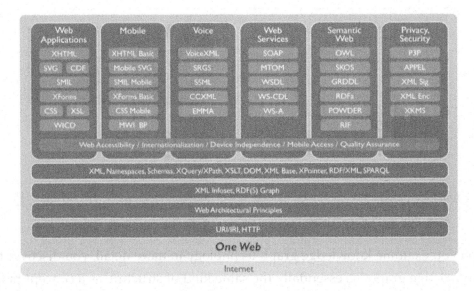

The basic data level can be illustrated with graphs. Here's an example of the level of RDF, in the style used by the W3C:

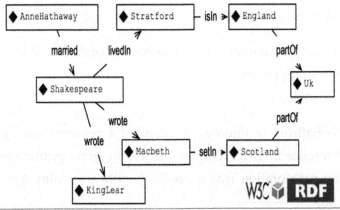

The diagram above is visualizing eight "triples," all in the form of sentences (for example, "Shakespeare wrote Macbeth"); the triples can be combined into the semantic network. The metadata level for RDF is called the "RDF Schema," and uses concepts such as types, properties, and sub-properties. So, England would be a country and *King Lear* a play. Working with structures like that, people (called "ontologists" when working in this field) or software (by way of text analysis) can set up precise definitions of semantics.

Note that "semantic web" standards (and the related "topic maps" standards) are being used heavily in "knowledge engineering" environments. Information science is crowded with people defining and using ontologies: technology-supported vocabularies that support complex logic to the level of being able to infer conclusions about complex scenarios. The logic implemented is very similar to that used in UML class diagrams. You can learn much more about Google's knowledge graph and those of its competitors...just Google it!

Google's Knowledge Graph is the first and the most prominent example of the serious impact of semantics on large-scale modern computing technology. It has drastically reduced the number of unnecessary, irrelevant page hits and generally improved the perceived intelligence of the Google search engine.

2.4.5. COGNITIVE COMPUTING EXAMPLE: SAFFRON

Semantics is not restricted to search contexts. There is a company currently working to combine semantics with:

- Modern cognitive computing (the successor of Artificial Intelligence)
- Raw computing power
- Graph technology.

The company is Saffron Technology. I attended a presentation by Saffron at the SmartData Conference in 2015. They are active in some public sectors, and their main case in the presentation was from the healthcare realm: a recommendation system of coverage.

The environment Saffron created is very dynamic, incorporating "instant learning." It is based on schema-free semantic graphs and non-parametric statistics. "Memories" are maintained by way of semantic connections in the graph, combined with statistical counts and conditional context. Much of the power of the reasoning (e.g. for building recommendations) is based on the concept of "similarity." What is the cognitive "distance," for example, to a similar item in the past? What was this item? What was done in that case, and with what outcome?

Saffron summarizes their big idea as being where natural intelligence (implemented as software) meets machine learning. Natural intelligence tries to mimic what we believe goes on inside our brains. We can assume that association is taking place, and some sort of contextual reasoning takes advantage of that. The learning process is autonomous. The newer technology of machine learning (also called "deep learning") is a brute force (hardware and software) approach that is driven by large amounts of data coming from multiple sources. The algorithms employed are frequently proprietary, and are based on statistics, non-linear approaches, semantics, "neural networks," and many more concepts.

Machine learning is in the big data space. It's no longer hidden by artificial intelligence researchers in universities or born-digital companies like Amazon,

Google, and Netflix. More importantly, it generates significant business value. Visit McKinsey for an example: http://bit.ly/1GLaOF4.

In summary, keep in mind two key points. First, remember that modern cognitive computing is based on increased understanding of neuroscience, of the structures involved in our perception and cognition, and of the most powerful computer of them all: the human brain. Second, understand that these technologies will continue to impact many areas of computing in the future (including data modeling, as you will see).

2.4.6. UBIQUITOUS POINTER

Pointing is a very basic gesture for humans.

http://bit.ly/29PoVjS by Hillebrand Steve, U.S. Fish and Wildlife Service [Public domain], via Wikimedia Commons

Nobody is in doubt about what the intention is, regardless of culture, language, or circumstance.

This is supported by sound science. Here is an abstract for an article in Developmental Review, Volume 30, Issue 4, December 2010, Pages 352–366, Authors: Cristina Colonnesia, Geert Jan J.M. Stamsa, Irene Kostera, Marc J. Noomb.

The use of the pointing gesture is one of the first ways to communicate with the world. This gesture emerges before the second year of life and it is assumed to be the

first form of intentional communication. This meta-analysis examined the concurrent and longitudinal relation between pointing and the emergence of language. Twenty-five studies were included into the meta-analysis, including 734 children. The role of several moderators was examined: pointing modality, pointing motive, age at which the pointing was measured, the assessment method of the pointing gesture and language development, the modality of language, socioeconomic status, and country. ... It is concluded that the pointing gesture is a key joint-attention behavior involved in the acquisition of language.

It's no coincidence, then, that objects called "pointers" have appeared in (and disappeared from) different data models for decades. (See chapter 2.)

Ted Codd, the inventor of the relational model, spent a lot of energy arguing against having pointers in databases. Admittedly, some of the physical implementations of pointers in Codd's time had some serious drawbacks. Collectively known as "the broken chain," pointers often pointed at the wrong places due to physical mishaps (like a power outage during an update of a chain of pointers).

Regardless of Codd's skepticism, pointers are here to stay. Today they proliferate corporate databases under the disguise of "surrogate keys." Nowadays, of course, the physical implementations are a lot better and more robust, backed up by indexes and key / value storage schemes. Tripping on a power cord isn't such a devastating experience.

The pointer is one of the strongest visualization tools in our possession. That's why I heavily favor directed graphs, such as concept maps.

2.4.7. THINK SPATIALLY

As detailed in the previous sections in this chapter, there seems to be serious value in leveraging concepts and conceptual spaces. Think spatially. Think in terms of locations and proximity. Think in context.

Here is an example of a person (John. F. Kennedy) and his personality profile (as per IBM Watson, based on JFK's inauguration speech):

Visualization of Personality Data

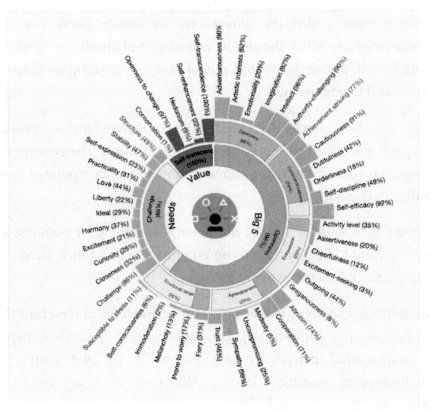

Source: http://bit.ly/1wXMi4D

Each of the axes in the diagram above represents a coordinate (for example Intellect 98%). Together those coordinates describe a location in the space, where the person is to be found; which describes the personality. The more dimensions you know (that is, the more context that you have), the more precisely you can determine what is in the location pointed to by the collection of dimensions. This is what both concept mapping and conceptual spaces are all about. The spatial metaphor is a very strong way to describe how the brain works under the perceptive process leading to cognition. You – intuitively – get the feeling "I know what this is about", which actually means that you have navigated the conceptual space (neural network) and located something in there. If you know it beforehand ("been there, done that"), the realization comes to you. If you "have not been there before", you might get fascinated about something new and potentially interesting; you might decide to "go there" to find out more.

What matters most is that the dimensions are clearly defined in an easily recognizable language, which the observers understand intuitively. That language, in the context of this book, is the data model as it is expressing itself towards the people who need to understand it.

Visualization has been a recognized need in data modeling for many years, but the particular style used matters more than one might think. The concept mapping style is a proven way of effective communication and is incorporated in our way of presenting data models.

Finally, pointing is another way of addressing something. If pointers were not effective, you would likely not use a computer mouse or a touch screen—both of these gestures are, in essence, ways of pointing.

The natural conclusion, then, is that visual representations of structure should be based on pointing (i.e. with arrows). This takes us back to concept maps, which from a mathematical perspective, are essentially directed graphs. Arrows undoubtedly support meaningful learning. When you develop a data model, you are an educator—always remember that!

The five guiding principles of modern visual communication of structure and content are:

Now that we understand how to best communicate with our readers, we can more closely consider our data modeling options.

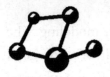

Chapter 3
Real Requirements of Data Modeling

Data modeling is about exploration and discovery. We go to unexplored (or under-explored) territories and try to elicit meaningful knowledge from the clues we find there. We are always looking for relationships and patterns, which convey the structure of the landscape that we tour. We then write our findings as maps for others to profit from, should they desire or need to follow in our footprints.

So, using this expedition metaphor, let us begin by asking some basic questions:

- Why should we do data modeling in the post-relational world while on our expedition?

- What are the observations of other travelers that have been there before us?

- Which skills and tools should the cartographer use when mapping the new territory?

3.1. POST-RELATIONAL DATA MODELING

Traditionally, data modeling has followed a process like this:

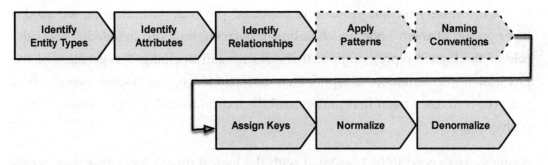

See Scott Ambler's good overview at: http://bit.ly/XALNgy

The first three activities are the classic processes associated with modeling. The next two (dotted) processes are quite useful, and are the hallmarks of good craftsmanship. The final three steps bring the modeler closer to the physical model. Conceptual modeling has faded away in favor of the "Great Pragmatic and Quick Unified Data Modeling Practice." Even in the legacy relational systems development universe, agility has moved up on the list of priorities, leaving conceptual modeling "on the bench."

If you zoom out a little, you see that the "unified" process is trying to accomplish two aspects of developing a good solution:

- Describing the "what" (in terms of a conceptual / logical data model)

- Describing some aspects of the "how" (e.g. physical access optimization via denormalization for better performance).

To truly understand this unified process, we first must get better at distinguishing between the "what" and the "how." In other words, we must understand that the conceptual-level model has a place independent of the solution-level and physical-level models. Second, we must realize that the logical data model is an artifact designed by people, not something given beforehand. It encompasses design decisions about scope, generalizations, abstractions, and aggregations. Finally, we must understand that the physical data model has a whole lot more emphasis in the NoSQL world than in the relational world.

Given the variety of data stores and mirrored physical data models, we need a layer on top of them—one which is business-facing and still detailed. This is the role of the logical representation. It should remain unchanged regardless of the physical implementation. Despite their independence, developers need a firm grasp of both; they must first understand the logical model in order to implement it physically.

Business users need to be presented with the logical model whenever they access the data in the system. Today, all kinds of data are targets for analytics; as such, they are not always protected by a home-made application containing rules and mappings to the business terminology.

This matches the best practice of using "user stories" for business / user level requirements. Deconstructing the user story is a conceptual-to-logical modeling process. The actual construction of the solution data model results in the logical data model layer in the middle. Underneath that follows (in a later process) the physical layer. This 3-layer architecture embraces user needs and terminology on one end, and the necessary physical data aspects on the other. The focus of this book is the logical data model, which really is a solution data model.

Ever since "sort/merge" was invented with the magnetic tape revolution in the 1950's, the need for data models has been evident. (For those of you who never worked with tape-based computing, understand that we actually built hierarchical data models on tape using "record type" fields to control the structure.)

In data modeling what we are looking for is meaning and structure. The whole purpose of the data model is to communicate the business meaning and the structure of the information, which describes the business contents of the database.

Meaning is really owned and defined by the business in question. They have the privilege of deciding on their own terminology, setting their own goals, and ultimately telling their own story. To effectively communicate these business stories, we first need to nail down the business semantics. There are a few different ways to accomplish this.

Structure is often defined by somebody else. When you describe a product, you have to describe physical aspects as well as some business aspects (price, maybe). If we are not talking about natural objects or events (such as animals, raw materials, the flow of water in a river, etc.), the objects are also designed by people. Understanding the structure is obviously necessary in order to grasp the significance and the context.

3.2. FINDING MEANING AND STRUCTURE

3.2.1. WORKING WITH BUSINESS PEOPLE

Data modeling has been around for many years, but it's still a work in progress. We have learned, after all, that one size does not fit all.

The growing realization is that relational DBMSs have their limits, and that other paradigms serve some circumstances better. Some of these circumstances in which DBMS might fail could be extremely high volumes (in which case key-values or Hadoop would better serve us) or highly complex data structures (in which case knowledge graphs and networks would be appropriate).

This realization gives us an opportunity to re-think how we support the data modeling process with all manner of thoughtful and productive data modeling practices. Wherever possible, we should strive to employ data modeling paradigms that work in different contexts and that provide an evolutionary path from the business level to the physical level.

But where to begin? Since these are business ventures, it's prudent to start by defining the stakeholders.

The well-known "RACI" matrix (as defined in the IIBA Business Analysis Book of Knowledge, http://www.iiba.org/babok-guide.aspx) describes the roles of those involved in business analysis activities. It describes stakeholders as having one or more of the following responsibilities for a given task or deliverable:

- [R]esponsible: does the work
- [A]ccountable: is the decision maker (only one stakeholder!)
- [C]onsulted: must be consulted for input
- [I]nformed: will be notified of the outcome.

Each of these categories has the potential to include many stakeholders:

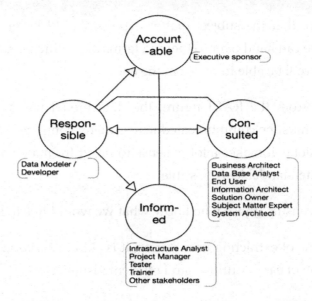

That is all well and fine, but the classic business analysis workflows are challenged because of rapid changes in:

- Requirement elicitation as user stories (not as formal specs)
- Project work styles (including iterative)
- New technologies, data stores, etc.
- Data governance "as you go"
- Data-driven analytics and big data.

The people, who are actively soliciting information (the producers of metadata and business process knowledge) are:

- business analysts
- subject matter experts
- data modelers
- developers.

The people contributing by way of consultation (sometimes called "the readers") are either business specialists (i.e. subject matter experts) or the system owner(s), plus various kinds of architects.

I honestly believe that the subject matter experts should be given a key role to play; the more we can hand over to them in terms of producing a user's stories, the better solutions we'll be able to create in the end.

As you can see from the RACI figure, the data model has a lot of "readers." Consequently, it must be communicated across many competencies and priorities. For that reason alone, it makes a lot of sense to profit from a data model, which is as intuitively understandable as possible.

So, how do we "consult" those who know what we would like to know?

This process is one of extracting user stories. It is akin to exploration, and must be supported by way of easy, intuitive, and efficient visualizations.

3.2.2. CONCEPT MODELS AS PART OF USER STORIES

Working with concept maps to extract user stories is a creative process. In my book from 2012 [5], I combine it with design principles to create a process with three areas of focus:

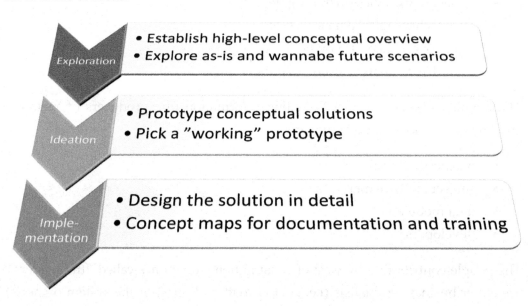

Exploration
- Establish high-level conceptual overview
- Explore as-is and wannabe future scenarios

Ideation
- Prototype conceptual solutions
- Pick a "working" prototype

Imple-mentation
- Design the solution in detail
- Concept maps for documentation and training

Further explained in Frisendal, T.: Design Thinking Business Analysis - Business Concept Mapping Applied, Thomas Frisendal, © Springer, 2012

Begin by exploring the subject area using rough concept maps. These are visual user stories, if you will. Then take the most promising of those stories and develop them into prototypes by adding detail. Finally, choose the solution that seems most promising and finish it up by adding details about all relationships and properties. This may require two to four workshops, each lasting a few hours. Be prepared to map the concepts on the fly using a data projector and CmapTools, or a similar product.

The resulting concept map is ready for transformation into a solution data model, as will be explained in the next chapter. Here are some questions and guidelines to get you thinking about how to transform your concept map into a working solution:

Where to look? Where is the knowledge about the business? Obviously there are a lot of potential sources:

- Inside peoples' minds
- In the business documents
- Inside operational documents such as charts of accounts, spreadsheets, IT data models and databases, and business intelligence reports.

Top-down or bottom-up? Doing a top-down deconstruction of the desired feature or information content is probably the most common pattern in designing user stories. However, it happens that you are driven by (legacy) data, in which case a re-engineering of the physical data model into a more business-friendly representation (concept model) is appropriate. You choose what is best. Sometimes a combination of the two works out fine.

Get the business pains out in the daylight! As you brainstorm your concept models in the preparation of user stories, you (and the business folks) do have some learning experiences. Expect some surprises. Here are some frequent discoveries:

- Our terminology is imprecise or arcane, perhaps born out of tradition
- Some of our concepts are plain wrong

- "Is this really what we are doing?"

and other such "aha moments."

Generalization is your friend. Frequently you run into challenges in handling complex contexts. By tradition, maybe, some business concepts have evolved into a "spaghetti" of too many concepts and relationships; not always in a coherent structure. It is indeed best practice to strive for simplicity. And your weapon in this situation is to generalize the structure that you see into a simpler structure using less but more general concepts. This is something you should always have in the back of your head. "Can we find a simple representation of this that provides the same or better business value?"

Start simple. Use circles for all concepts in the beginning, when you are brainstorming or sketching a map.

Identify relationships. Very clearly name all the relations between concepts. Make sure everyone is on the same page about the terminology used.

- **One-to-one relationships.** Use a connecting line without an arrowhead to denote a one-to-one relationship between concepts.

- **One-to-many relationships.** Use a connecting line with an arrowhead at the "many" side to denote a one-to-many relation between two business objects.

- **Many-to-many relationships.** Carefully check whether there really is no business object in the middle of a many-to-many relation. If it is truly missing, use a connecting line with an arrowhead in each end.

Objects and properties. In later stages of the modeling flow, circles represent "business objects" (or entity types). Rounded rectangles represent properties (or attributes, in classic data modeling) of objects.

Sample data. You may, at times, use squared rectangles to denote actual values (of data) for pedagogical purposes. Not all readers know all the concepts. So, in an attempt to explain, you could add some real data in the concept model. In section 2.4.2, you see "Fuel type" explained by visualizing some sample data like "Gasoline", "Electricity" and "LPG".

When to stop? Somewhere there is a border between the data model and business rules. Business rules tend to include specific data, whereas data models don't. So, if you find that you are including data in the diagrams, do not do it, except for pedagogical reasons, maybe. Detailed rules should exist as textual descriptions, not as diagrams. Business rules should not reside within a data model, but may be kept in a separate document or a business rule elicitation tool.

Top-down page layout. Concept maps should be easy to read. Psychologists have shown that readers expect a top-down organization of the map.

These activities happen at this stage of the life-cycle:

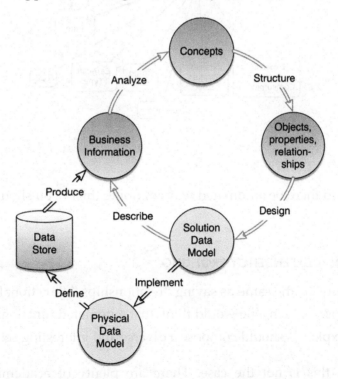

Here is an example concept map from the world of shipping. It is a snapshot of a work in progress (the freight rates, for instance, still need to be elaborated):

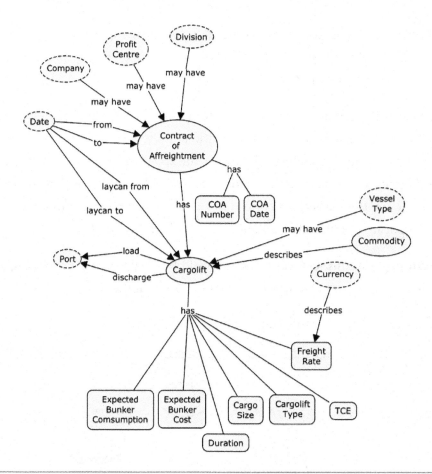

Further examples can be found in Frisendal, T.: Design Thinking Business Analysis - Business Concept Mapping Applied, Thomas Frisendal, © Springer, 2012

"But wait! Could there be automated ways of doing this?" you should ask. What if we ask the data?

3.2.3. FUNCTIONAL DEPENDENCY PROFILING

Saying "structure" is the same as saying "relationships." Functional dependencies are relationships. As such, one would think that automated functional dependency checkers and explorers should compose a diverse and interesting set of tools.

Unfortunately, this is not the case. There are plenty of academic papers and projects on the topic, but on the commercial side, there is not a whole lot. Inside the big data modeling tools, you can find some.

In the early 2000's, tools that actually look in depth at your data started to emerge. People realized that data always speaks for itself. Inside the data, you will find the truth about all the dependencies that are actually contained in them.

The products doing this are called "data profiling tools." They are designed to catch all information about data by way of actually reading through them. A report containing the meta data is the result. Here is a definition from Wikipedia:

> *Data profiling is an analysis of the candidate data sources for a data warehouse to clarify the structure, content, relationships and derivation rules of the data. Profiling helps not only to understand anomalies and to assess data quality, but also to discover, register, and assess enterprise metadata. Thus the purpose of data profiling is both to validate metadata when it is available and to discover metadata when it is not.*

https://en.wikipedia.org/wiki/Data_profiling

Data profiling software can be used to spot many things. In the context of data modeling we are very interested in learning more about:

- Potential inter-table relationships (also called foreign key relationships)

- Potential intra-table relationships (also called functional dependencies).

Let us suppose that we are looking at a database that contains "Product No" in one table and "Item No" in another table. It a good assumption that they refer to the same concept. We can ask that of the data profiling software by doing both inter- and intra-table matches of occurrences of the two sets of values. If Product No on the Orderlines matches Item No on the Items table, for example, there is some support for the assumption that we are looking at a (inter-table) relationship. The number of unmatched vs. the number of matched values determine the quality of the relationship. If, for example 95 % are match, it is very likely an intended relationship. But if the only 40 % match the assumption has not been proven with any certainty. A classic Venn diagram can visualize this:

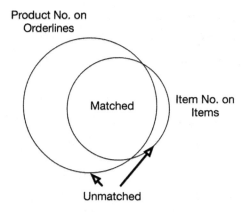

Product No. on
Orderlines

Matched

Item No. on
Items

Unmatched

If the percentage of unmatched results is too high, the probability that you are looking at a significant real-life relationship is low.

This is quite useful. As a data warehouse modeler, I have been faced with the task of modeling a legacy system with highly undocumented physical data models (employing 12-character data names, and the like). Data profiling can provide help in understanding the data structures in the bowl of data that you are looking at.

Most of the profiling tools I have seen work from a "quality" measure; the strength of the relationship between two sets of keys in one, two, or more tables is set to 100%, if everything on one side matches the other side perfectly. What brings down the strength of the relationship is unmatched keys on either side. If the potential relationship is from A to B, it reduces the quality of the relationship. If there are values in B which are not matched in A, this could be a problem. That could mean Orderlines regarding unknown products. The other way around is more acceptable—it means unordered Products.

Consider another example, which is on the intra-table level: You are examining the result of a functional dependency check within a product table. It shows that there is a dependency between ProductSubCategoryID and Style. However, it has a quality of 95%, because there are violations. For one, the Style = "U" is found in four different ProductSubCategoryIDs; as such, the functional dependency does not hold completely. However, 95% match is a good starting point; somebody will have to clean up the 5% dirty data.

Most data profiling tools will indicate which rows support the relationship and which rows violate it.

If this had been the first time you visited that database, you would probably not know which level in the product hierarchy determined Style. After profiling the data, you not only know this, but you also know that there are data quality problems. One check with a data profiling tool has revealed a lot of useful information.

There are plenty of data profiling tools available in all varieties: open source, commercial, standalone, and as components of ETL and data integration products.

But can we do better? What about machine learning?

3.2.4. MINING THE SEMANTICS

There are even better technologies that can actively help you to distill the concepts and relationships in a given body of data.

Knowledge engineers and information scientists have for years employed tools for mining structured and unstructured data, in order to extract both data and metadata. Look for methods and tools within text analytics for things like:

- Data level:
  - (Named) entity extraction (data level, persons, companies, products)
  - Sentiment analysis
  - Text mining

- Metadata level:
  - Concept extraction / mining
  - Relationship, fact, and event recognition
  - Classification of documents.

Obviously, we as data modelers are mostly interested in extracting metadata in the form of concepts and relationships, which can be fed right into our data models.

Much of the above is document-centric, focusing on unstructured or semi-structured data. Frequently the word "modeling" is used more in the sense of data mining or statistical modeling than in the sense of data modeling. However, understanding the concepts and relationships is equally important whether you are a data scientist or a data modeler/developer.

Text analysis and analytics are heavy-duty technologies which incorporate sets of semantic/linguistic, statistical, and machine learning techniques.

In 2015, one of the information management old-timers, Informatica, released the "Live Data Map 1.0." It is an impressive offering, which is positioned as a knowledge graph of all enterprise metadata, incorporating (among many other things) functionality for:

- Semantic Search with intelligent facets
- Related data assets
- Semantic content through data domains
- Business lineage
- Business glossary
- Relationship discovery.

These metadata points are continuously updated across the Informatica platform, for governance, data preparation, data extraction, and similar purposes.

At the end of the day, the most important function is relationship discovery. Understanding business semantics is closely related to understanding the structures of relationships, including dependencies. Discovery works by detecting the quality of cross-business object type relationships, as described above in the discussion of data profiling. There are two desired functionalities within relationship discovery:

- Automated suggestions of relationships (and accompanying keys)
- Visualization of relationships.

A new generation of data profiling vendors (including Paxata, Trifacta, and Tamr) are marching out in force these days as part of the big data and analytics space, with similar offerings based on semantics and machine learning. They are referred to as "data preparation vendors," and they employ the same kinds of heavy-duty tools within areas such as:

- Data discovery
- Data transformation
- Data modeling / structuring
- Metadata catalogs.

They typically also offer workspaces, designed to be used interactively by business analysts (data scientists) using visual tools.

The Gartner Group has looked at these new data preparation vendors in some detail; they have compiled a "Market Guide for Self-Service Data Preparation for Analytics."

If you let the data analysts do such machine-assisted data modeling without governance, you run a considerable risk of (A) getting more than one version of the truth, and/or (B) repeating modeling work that has already been done by somebody else.

You cannot model data in isolation from everything else. There is bound to be some overlap and you also need to integrate with other data in other systems or databases. You need to compare your data with other data, designed by somebody else in a different context and maybe some time ago. And this is what data models are for: learning from your new data model and comparing it with other models, discovered by other people.

Automate as much as you can, but have business people inside the loop in order to validate and consolidate the findings and the resulting data models. Visualization is a robust and quick way to achieve this validation.

3.3. Visualization of Models

3.3.1. FUNCTIONAL DEPENDENCY VISUALIZATION

One of the major contributions of Dr. Ted Codd's relational model is the focus on the importance of functional dependencies. In fact, normalization is driven by a modeler's desire for a relation where strict functional dependency applies across all the binary relations between the designated primary key and the fields depending on it.

As such, functional dependencies are very important contributors to the structural description of the information being modeled.

Inter-table dependencies are modeled as relationships; depending on the declarative language (e.g. SQL) they may be named (with a "constraint name") or not.

Intra-table dependencies, on the other hand, are not present in the relational model. The only indication of their presence is the logical co-location in the table of the fields, which are guaranteed (by the data modeler) to be functionally dependent on the primary key and that alone. No arrows, no names, no nothing.

Since dependencies between data are key to creating a correct data model, we need to bring the dependencies out into the bright sun. They must be clearly explicated, like this pedagogical functional dependency graph on the facing page.

Unfortunately, not many people have worked with functional dependencies on the visual level as Bob Dewhurst does in the graph on the facing page.

In his seminal book "Introduction to Database Systems, Volume I" [2], C.J. Date creates little "FD diagrams" that show the relationships between attributes in relations. The attributes are each in small rectangles (similar to concept maps), but the relationships are not named.

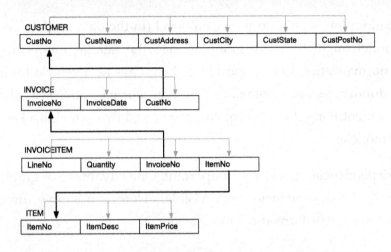

Inspired by online learning pages from Charles Darwin University, Bob Dewhurst (http://blt.ly/29XOVvD)

Beyond functional dependencies, other spill-overs from normalization include avoiding redundancies and update anomalies. Date's famous supplier-parts example illustrates this:

SNO	SNAME	STATUS	CITY
S1	Smith	20	London
S2	Jones	30	Paris
S3	Blake	30	Paris
S4	Clark	20	London
S5	Adams	30	Athens

This is in second normal form, which implies that it could contain redundancy (of city, for example). It also implies an update anomaly; it is impossible to register a city before you have a supplier in that city. City and Supplier are more independent than dependent. Supplier No (SNO) is not an identifying key for Cities. Yes, there is a relationship between Supplier and City, but having them in the same relation is not a good idea, because it hides important structural information (the relationship between supplier and city).

This relation is ill-defined because not all of its fields are functionally dependent on the same key. So, what the cookbook recipe of normalization is doing is identifying which relations (tables) are not well-formed (according to the mathematics behind the paradigm used by Dr. Ted Codd in his relational model).

Since the co-location is only on the visual level (in the data model), and since the physical model might be more granular than the tabular model (e.g. a graph database), normalization loses importance these days as a vehicle for eliminating physical redundancies and anomalies. However, normalization was also designed to help with identifying the inherent structures, and that remains a key obligation of the data modeler.

Detecting dependencies is still very important. One advantage of graph databases is that they make dependencies very visible. Here is a simple directed graph representation of the ill-formed relation above:

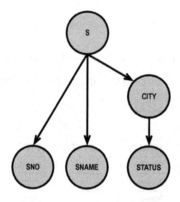

Visualization of functional dependencies is certainly a business requirement of data modeling. It's a powerful tool for detecting dependencies and many more processes.

We have drawn diagrams over the last 40 years or more, but not all of them were highly communicative, as we have seen in chapter 2. The diagrams that we have been using, are actually drawn by engineers (data modelers) in order to be shown to other engineers (developers). That is all fine and well. In fact, UML and ER models work fine for programming tasks. But for business facing modeling tasks, they are too complex. We need simplicity. And we need visualization.

3.3.2. UNDERSTANDING STRUCTURE AND CONTENT

If communication is our challenge, visualization is our solution.

To reflect a bit on the challenges that the relational model brought upon us, I will first turn your attention to the term "relation."

What the term implies (loosely) is that the relation is a set of binary relations, and if all those relations are functionally dependent on the same function, the functional relation of all of the set members (or columns) is good to go. This relation will be stamped as properly normalized. Many people think "relationship" when they hear the term "relation." And in terms of everyday semantics, that is perfectly right. For data modelers though, structure rules the world.

And structure is not handled well, at least visually in the classic relational model. Relationships are secondary citizens of relational. They are normally not named at all in the visualizations, and functional dependencies (i.e. the sources of meaning / semantics) are not visible or named. This goes for both inter-table and intra-table dependencies.

Our previous approaches to conceptual modeling, based on simplified entity-relationship diagrams or UML class diagram style visualizations did not communicate a lot of information to the business people. Normally they were very general and typically used for the one-page overview. The overview has its role, but it is not a business information structure diagram.

Concept maps, such as the example on the following page, communicate information structure extremely efficiently, and they're easy to produce.

Notice the named relationships, which include the functional dependencies (for example, employee and salary), and notice how you can read the whole thing in short sentences. Imagine the same thing expressed as text. Surely, the concept map communicates clearly and quickly. But there is a drawback. While they're more succinct than text-based user stories, though, they can still quickly become daunting in size. Can we find a more compact representation?

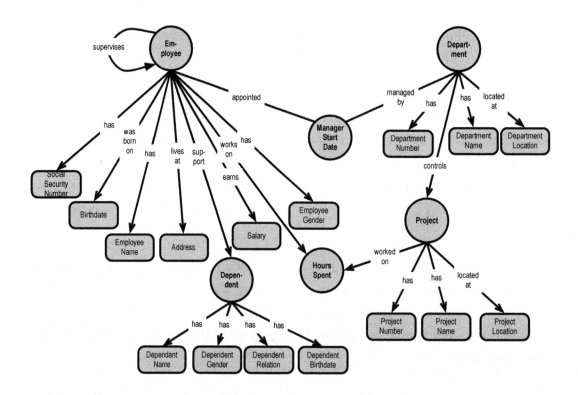

3.3.3. PROPERTY GRAPHS

We have looked at, what we can do to visualize structure. Let us now worry about content.

Given that structure is important, why then, do the classic data modeling practices all deliver content diagrams much like the model on the facing page, on the "logical" level?

The diagram above is filled with detail:

- Tables and their names
- All of the fields and their data types
- Primary keys and foreign keys (named by their constraint names)
- Relationships as "crow's feet" with either dashed lines or full lines, signaling "mandatory" or "optional".

The needed detail is present, but most of the space is used for listing table content (i.e. field lists).

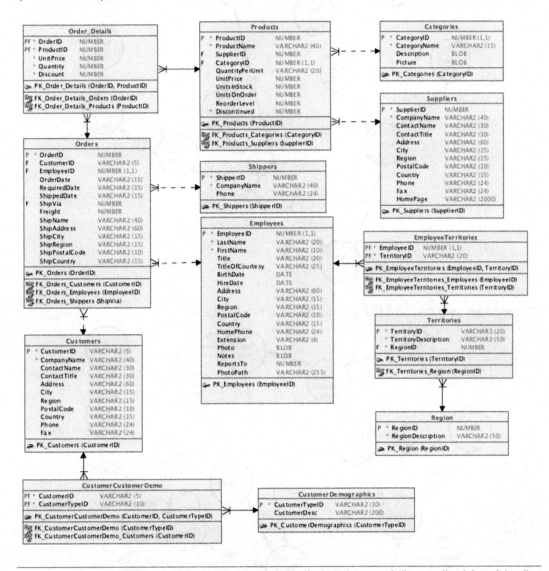

Slightly simplified diagram built from the Microsoft Northwind documentation on the internet by the author using Oracle SQL Developer Data Modeler

Property graphs are directed graphs, just like concept maps, and they offer elegant visualization of structure, such as the example on the facing page.

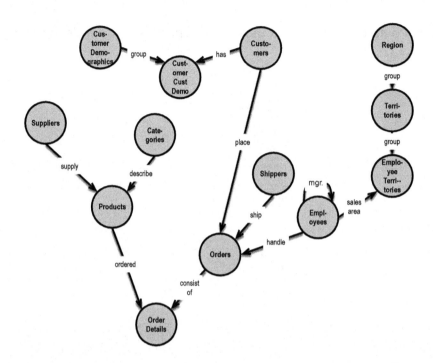

If necessary, we can add the properties discretely like this:

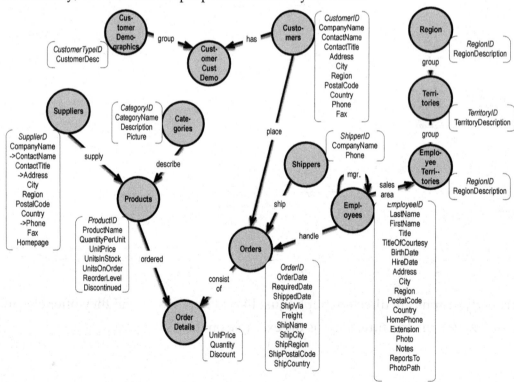

Not all of the details about the data model are found in the diagram above, but we really do not need to have all details on all diagrams, always.

Properties of a business type are all at the same "location" by definition. It logically follows that the business object types are the "landmarks" of the data model. One size does not fit all. But property graphs come close to being the perfect candidates for a database-agnostic representation of data models.

Property graphs are similar to concept maps in that there is no normative style (e.g. like there is in UML). So feel free to find your own style. If you communicate well with your readers, you have accomplished the necessary.

3.3.4. PROGRESSIVE VISUALIZATION OF DATA MODELS

Graphs are powerful, also on the data level. Here is an example from the Linked Data organization (http://linkeddata.org).

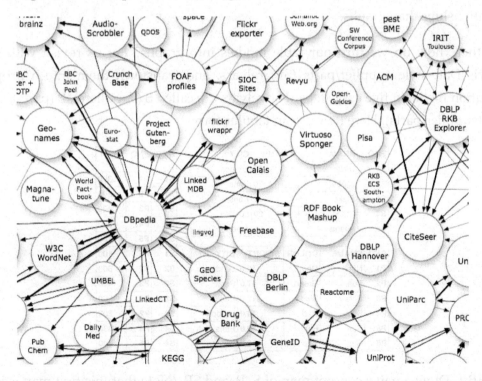

Part of a huge graph found on the Linked Data website; Creative Commons license

The linked data movement has been around for some years now, and it is still growing. Here are their own words about what they do:

> Linked data is about using the Web to connect related data that wasn't previously linked, or using the Web to lower the barriers to linking data currently linked using other methods. Specifically, Wikipedia defines "linked data" as "A term used to describe a recommended best practice for exposing, sharing, and connecting pieces of data, information, and knowledge on the Semantic Web using URIs and RDF."

Source: http://linkeddata.org

In short, graphs represent complex relationships between data occurrences (nodes), in many different dimensions for all permutations, for which there are data. This is indeed, from a mathematical point of view, a large directed graph: a network of interconnected data. Also for data models, relationships play key roles in models (structure is what it is about!), and there is no better way to represent relationships than graphs.

So then, how do we turn our table models into graphs? Let us revisit with the Chris Date-style supplier/parts (SP) relvars, and transform them into a proper solution model in five easy steps. The relvars are called S (suppliers), P (parts), and SP (supplier/parts). Here they are, in tabular form:

SNO	SNAME	STATUS	CITY
S1	Smith	20	London
S2	Jones	30	Paris
S3	Blake	30	Paris
S4	Clark	20	London
S5	Adams	30	Athens

PNO	PNAME	COLOR	WEIGHT	CITY
P1	Nut	Red	12.0	London
P2	Bolt	Green	17.0	Paris
P3	Screw	Blue	17.0	Paris
P4	Screw	Red	14.0	London
P5	Can	Blue	12.0	Paris
P6	Cog	Red	19.0	London

SNO	PNO	QTY
S1	P1	300
S1	P2	200
S1	P3	400
S1	P4	200
S1	P5	100
S1	P6	100
S2	P1	300
S2	P2	400
S3	P2	200
S4	P2	200
S4	P4	300
S4	P5	400

STEP 1: Draw a naive concept map of S, P, and SP. (Note that this first map is just to get us started; no particular symbolism is needed in the representation yet.)

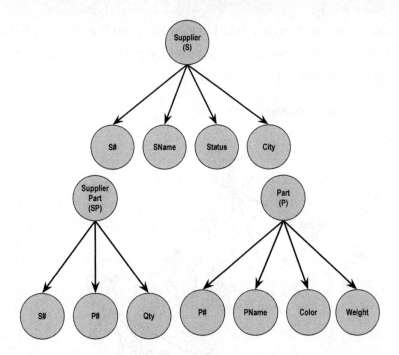

STEP 2: Visualize the relationships between S, P, and SP:

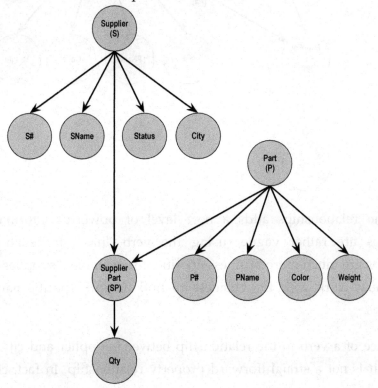

There is indeed a many-to-many relationship between S and P—only carrying the Qty as information. The foreign keys of supplier-part are S# and P#, because they are the identities of S and P, respectively.

STEP 3: Name the relationships:

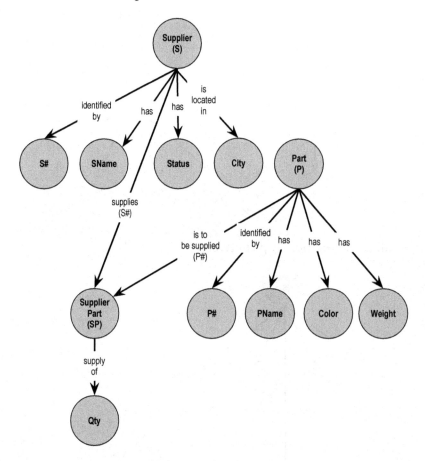

Naming the relationships adds a new level of powerful information. Some relationships are rather vague (using the verb "has," for example). Other relationships are much more business-specific (for example, "supplies.") The data modeler must work with the business to find helpful, specific names for the relationships.

The presence of a verb in the relationship between supplier and city could well mean that it is not a straightforward property relationship. In fact, cities do not share identity with suppliers; suppliers are located in cities. (This is how to resolve functional dependencies.)

STEP 4: Resolving the functional dependency of city:

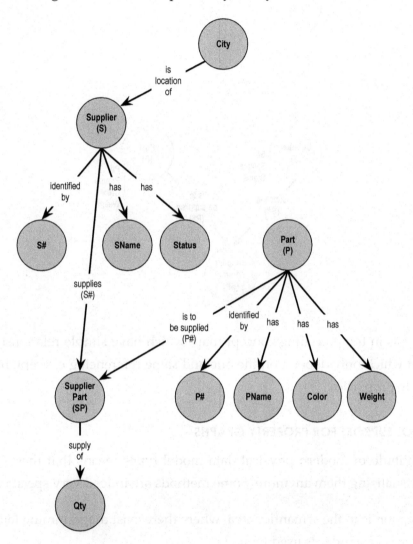

STEP 5: Reducing to a property graph data model, as shown on the next page.

Concepts, which are demonstrably the end nodes of (join) relationships between business objects, have been marked in bold. These were originally highlighted in the relationship name ("identified by"). This bold notation corresponds to C. J.

Date's original syntax in his presentations, where the primary key columns had a double underscore under the attribute name.

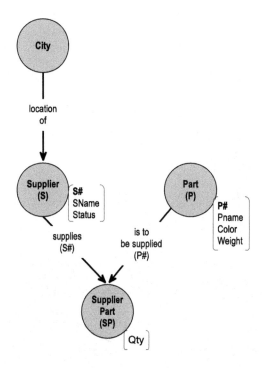

All concepts in the preceding concept map, which have simple relationships (has, is...), and which only depend on the one and same referencing concept, have been reduced to properties.

3.3.5. TOOL SUPPORT FOR PROPERTY GRAPHS

The plentitude of modern physical data model types means that there is no one way of visualizing them anymore. Some methods are indeed very specific.

One exception is in the semantics area, where there exist diagramming facilities for the XML-based standards used there.

Surprisingly, there are no "ivy league" data modeling tools available for using property graphs to represent data model designs. The graph DBMS vendors do have some graph browsing tools, but many of them are too generic for our purposes. On the other end of the spectrum, there are some quite sophisticated graph visualization tools available for doing graph-based data analysis.

I figure that the "ivy league" data modeling tool vendors simply have to catch up. While they are at it, why not go 3D? Who will be the first?

Fortunately, we are not completely without means.

3.3.5.1 White-boarding on Tablets

Several of the use cases for data modeling processes are in the explorative and ideation phases. In these situations, you need a lot of "white board" space. This may not be a physical white board, though. The modern tablets have good support for "assisted" white-boarding.

One of the successful products is Paper from Fifty Three (www.fiftythree.com). It runs on iPhones and iPads. You will probably find a stylus helpful for tablet white-boarding. Paper includes some bright assistance (originally called Think Kit), which is now included in the free product. (The stylus is not free, but alternatives do exist.) Your drawings look good, because the software corrects your sloppy drawing style. Check out the videos on the internet.

Paper can produce diagrams like this at the speed of thought:

3.3.5.2 Diagramming tools

The visual meta-models for property graphs as data modeling paradigms are rather simple and easy to set up using Omnigraffle or Visio.

Here is the style I used in Omnigraffle to make some of the diagrams used in this book:

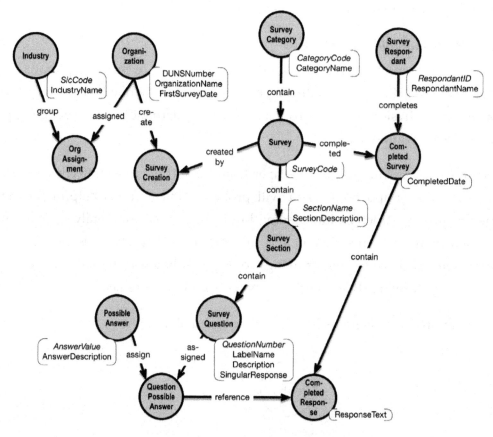

The example above (a survey form) is explained further in section 5.3. Omnigraffle is quite easy and does not require many clicks.

3.3.5.3 CmapTools

As previously discussed, I use the product CmapTools from IHMC for concept mapping. It is very easy to use, and you can draw as you go in a brainstorming session. You are not limited to the concept mapping style that I propose. The diagrams can be tweaked in many ways, and the tool is very productive.

Here is a little concept map style diagram drawn in CmapTools:

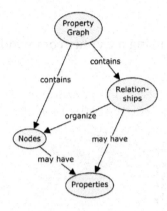

The diagram describes the structure of the property graph data model (simplified). CmapTools is available from this website http://cmap.ihmc.us. Please note that the basic IHMC CmapTools software is free for educational institutions and US Federal Government Agencies, and at this time the software is being offered free as a beta test version to other users, including commercial users.

3.3.5.4 Graph database browsers

The graph database products typically offer a browser as part of their user interface. Neo4j is one of the most popular graph databases in the NoSQL space (www.neo4j.com). A community edition is available for download. There are several ways of getting data into Neo4j. One way is to use a batch load from a CSV-file. You could collect the nodes (concepts) in an Excel sheet and load them into Neo4j using its Cypher query language. The Excel sheet should look like this:

ObjectID	Name	ObjectType	Property1	Property2	Property3	Property4
100	CompletedResponse	BusinessObject	ResponseText			
101	CompletedSurvey	BusinessObject	CompletedDate			
102	Industry	BusinessObject	SICCode	IndustryName		
103	Organization	BusinessObject	DUNSNumber	OrganizationName	FirstSurveyDate	
104	OrgAssignment	BusinessObject				
105	PossibleAnswer	BusinessObject	AnswerValue	AnswerDescription		
106	QuestionPossibleAnswer	BusinessObject				
107	Survey	BusinessObject	SurveyCode			
108	SurveyCategory	BusinessObject	CategoryCode	CategoryName		
109	SurveyCreation	BusinessObject				
110	SurveyQuestion	BusinessObject	QuestionNumber	LabelName	Description	SingularResponse
111	SurveyRespondent	BusinessObject	RespondantID	RespondantName		
112	SurveySection	BusinessObject	SectionName	SectionDescription		

The above node definitions are actually the nodes of the survey data model shown earlier in this chapter.

The load would be executed using a Cypher command like the following:

```
// Create BusinessObjects
LOAD CSV WITH HEADERS FROM "file:///SurveyMetadata.csv" AS row
CREATE (n:BusinessObject {ObjectID: row.ObjectID, Name: row.Name,
    ObjectType: row.ObjectType,
Property1: row.Property1,
Property2: row.Property2,
Property3: row.Property3,
Property4: row.Property4,
Property5: row.Property5,
Property6: row.Property6,
Property7: row.Property7,
Property8: row.Property8,
Property9: row.Property9,
Property10: row.Property10
})
```

One way of getting the edges (relationships) into Neo4j could be the following Cypher commands:

```
MATCH (a:BusinessObject), (b:BusinessObject) WHERE a.Name =
    'Industry' and b.Name = 'OrgAssignment' CREATE (a)-[:group]->(b)
MATCH (a:BusinessObject), (b:BusinessObject) WHERE a.Name =
    'Organization' and b.Name = 'OrgAssignment' CREATE (a)-
    [:assigned]->(b)
MATCH (a:BusinessObject), (b:BusinessObject) WHERE a.Name =
    'Organization' and b.Name = 'SurveyCreation' CREATE (a)-
    [:create]->(b)
MATCH (a:BusinessObject), (b:BusinessObject) WHERE a.Name = 'Survey'
    and b.Name = 'SurveyCreation' CREATE (a)-[:createdby]->(b)
MATCH (a:BusinessObject), (b:BusinessObject) WHERE a.Name =
    'SurveyCategory' and b.Name = 'Survey' CREATE (a)-[:contain]-
    >(b)
MATCH (a:BusinessObject), (b:BusinessObject) WHERE a.Name = 'Survey'
    and b.Name = 'SurveySection' CREATE (a)-[:contain]->(b)
MATCH (a:BusinessObject), (b:BusinessObject) WHERE a.Name = 'Survey'
    and b.Name = 'CompletedSurvey' CREATE (a)-[:completed]->(b)
```

```
MATCH (a:BusinessObject), (b:BusinessObject) WHERE a.Name =
    'SurveyRespondent' and b.Name = 'CompletedSurvey' CREATE (a)-
    [:completes]->(b)
MATCH (a:BusinessObject), (b:BusinessObject) WHERE a.Name =
    'QuestionPossibleAnswer' and b.Name = 'CompletedResponse' CREATE
    (a)-[:reference]->(b)
MATCH (a:BusinessObject), (b:BusinessObject) WHERE a.Name =
    'CompletedSurvey' and b.Name = 'CompletedResponse' CREATE (a)-
    [:assigned]->(b)
MATCH (a:BusinessObject), (b:BusinessObject) WHERE a.Name =
    'SurveyQuestion' and b.Name = 'QuestionPossibleAnswer' CREATE
    (a)-[:group]->(b)
MATCH (a:BusinessObject), (b:BusinessObject) WHERE a.Name =
    'PossibleAnswer' and b.Name = 'QuestionPossibleAnswer' CREATE
    (a)-[:group]->(b)
MATCH (a:BusinessObject), (b:BusinessObject) WHERE a.Name =
    'SurveySection' and b.Name = 'SurveyQuestion' CREATE (a)-
    [:contain]->(b)
```

Having the property graph data model in the Neo4j graph store enables you to browse it using the standard browser in the base product:

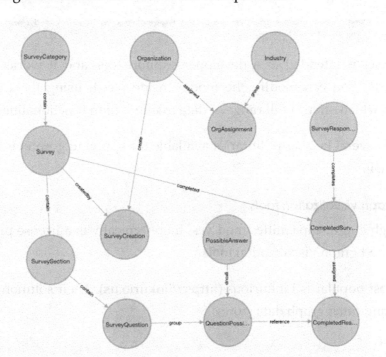

The properties of the individual nodes are available below the graph, if you click one of the nodes to highlight it:

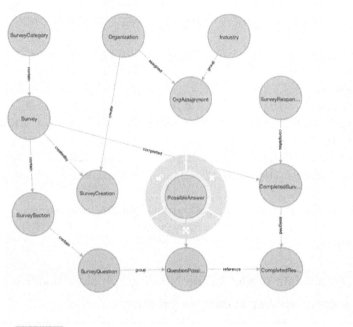

BusinessObject   <id>: 5   Property4:   ObjectType: BusinessObject   Property3:   Property2: AnswerDescription   Property1: AnswerValue
Property7:   Property6:   Property5:   Name: PossibleAnswer

The browser is intended as a developer support tool, and it works for all your basic needs. You can modify the model inside Neo4j using the Cypher query language, which offers a full range of data manipulation functionalities.

There are several JavaScript libraries available for applying graph visualization on top of Neo4j.

3.3.5.5 Graph visualization tools

At the high end of capabilities (and yes, there typically is a license price) we find sophisticated graph visualization tools.

Of the most popular is Linkurious (https://linkurio.us). Their solution runs on top of Neo4j and other graph data stores.

Linkurious offers a JavaScript toolkit (linkurious.js) for building graph exploration applications yourself. But they also offer a sophisticated, out of the box solution (which comes with a commercial license).

The same property graph data model as shown above can be presented like this in Linkurious:

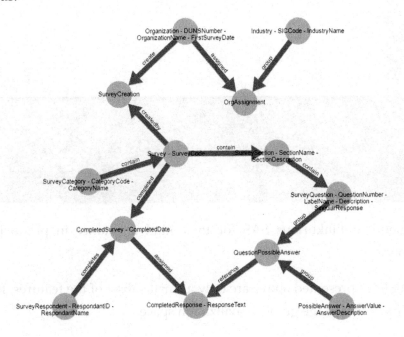

The graph is a bit compressed because of the little space available on a printed page in a book. The user interface on the screen is very usable indeed. Through the user interface you can add, modify, and delete nodes in your property graph data model:

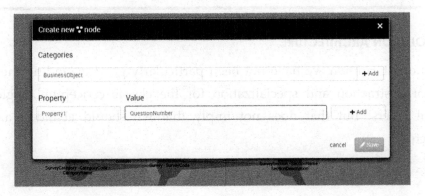

You can also add, modify, and delete edges in your data model:

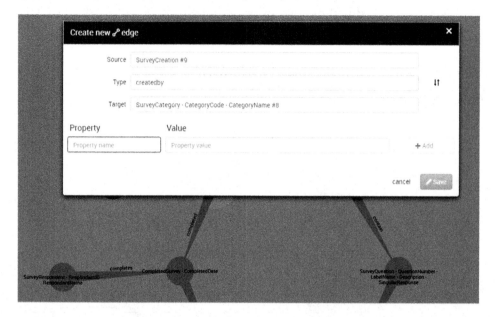

I am grateful to Linkurious SAS for their kind assistance in producing these screenshots.

The possibilities presented above are only a small subset of the features, functions, and vendors found in the graph visualization space.

Now we are ready to examine the "Requirements Specification" for data modeling.

3.4. DATA MODELING REQUIREMENTS

3.4.1. SOLUTION ARCHITECTURE

In my honest opinion we have not been particularly good at finding the proper levels of abstraction and specialization for the classic conceptual, logical and physical layers. But that does not imply that we should abandon a 3-layer architecture.

There is no doubt that on top we have a business-facing layer, which is based on knowledge elicitation by and from the business people. I prefer to call that the Business Concept Model layer.

The middle layer serves the purpose of containing the actual design of a solution to be implemented. It should ideally be subsetted from the business concept model and then extended with design decisions based on desired behaviors. I call that the Solution Data Model.

And finally, the good old Physical Data Model, as you would expect. The thing that is a transformation of the solution data model, and that a data store / DBMS can employ. This gives rise to this architecture of the Data Modeling system:

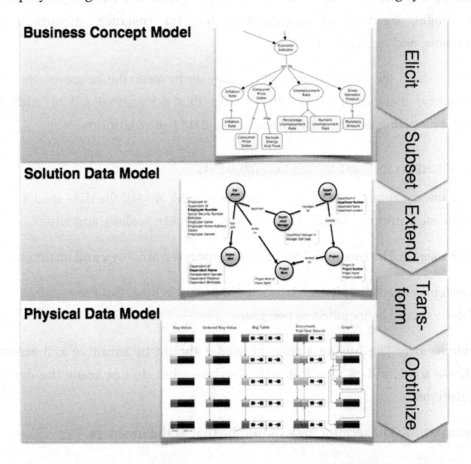

For a readable version of the illustration on the physical model level, see page 171.

As we begin to compile our list of data modeling requirements, this proposed layering of data models leads to these architecture level requirements:

Requirement 1: **A three-level data model architecture.**

Requirement 2: **The business-facing level must be built on a concept model paradigm (for visualization and effective learning).**

Requirement 3: **The solution-level data model is independent of the data store platform, and is derived from the concept-level model.**

Requirement 4: **The physical-level data model is specific to the data store platform, but the content should be easily mapped back to the solution-level data model, by way of visualization (of, for instance, denormalization, collections, and aggregates).**

Unfortunately, the physical modeling stage is beyond the scope of this book. Fortunately, there exist many other books that do a great job of addressing physical modeling aspects in their respective data store platforms.

3.4.2. BUSINESS CONCEPT MODEL REQUIREMENTS

The Business Concept Model is the business-facing side of the data model. This is pure business information, and is concerned with terminology and structure.

Requirement 5: **The business level must support terminology and structure.**

No system-related design decisions should be made here. But *business level* design decisions should be included as necessary.

Requirement 6: **The business concept model should be intuitive and accessible for those stakeholders who know the business, but do not know the details of IT solutions.**

Requirement 7: **The terminology should be that of the business.**

Requirement 8: **The business concept model should be easy to produce and maintain.**

A brainstorming work style is the typical elicitation process; there should be tool support for this task.

Requirement 9: **There should be visualization tools available for concept modeling, and they should be easy for business people to use.**

(Optional) Requirement 10: **Automated elicitation procedures may be employed (such as text mining and machine learning).**

Identity is not explicit, but uniqueness is implied by the references coming into the concept. This is because identity (more about that later) is frequently designed into the solution, whereas uniqueness is typically derived from a (combination of) business "keys." The uniqueness criteria may be a bit vague on the business level, which warrants a designed solution for obtaining guaranteed unique identities (because that is what we can handle in IT solutions).

The following concepts should be supported:

Requirement 11: **Business Objects.**

Requirement 12: **Properties of business objects.**

Requirement 13: **Atomic values (for illustration purposes).**

Requirement 14: **Named, directed relationships with simple cardinalities.**

Requirement 15: **A directed style for relationships between business objects.**

Requirement 16: **An undirected style for relationships between a business object and its properties.**

Requirement 17: **Generic data types (e.g., number, string, date, amount).**

Requirement 18: **Definitions of the terminology used (word lists with explanations and examples).**

Requirement 19: **Simple business rules written as text.**

The Concept Model will consist of overview models and of detailed subject area-specific models, as necessary.

The scope of the model may define the scope of the solution, but that is its only direct relationship to the next layer.

Requirement 20: **The Business Concept Models should be (at least) approved by the business people, including the sponsors.**

Obviously, this spins off a whole lot of functional requirements, but a good concept mapping tool supplemented with Excel sheets and Word lists will do quite well.

3.4.3. SOLUTION DATA MODEL REQUIREMENTS

What are the business reasons for creating a data model?

There are some categories of modelers:

- **The Explorer**: You are lucky; you develop a data model for a previously un-modeled subject area. No one in your organization has ever exploited this territory before. Wow!

- **The Integrator**: You are assigned the task of wrangling some data that was created by a system not developed by your organization, trying to whip the data into shape for integration with some of your own operational data. Good luck!

- **The Data Scientist**: You need to explore a lake of data, most of which is generated by exotic systems not homegrown in your own organization. May the force be with you!

These three modeling roles all share a strong requirement for being aligned with the business. This means talking the language of the business.

Maybe the Integrator is protected a bit, because they do not necessarily have to expose their solution data model. But they really need to understand the business terminology, and they must map the technical names of the implementation model to the business names of the solution model.

The general, high-level requirements of the solution data model can be expressed as follows:

> *We all need to communicate in the language of the business. Which translates into a need for doing a solution data model. Much of this book is about transforming data modeling from a rather technical and somewhat clerical discipline into a practice that is easy to perform, easy to understand and looks good. The focus should be on good craftsmanship. As you have seen already we have eliminated a lot of arcane complexity by simply going to a graph representation of the conceptual model, the concept maps. The solution data model continues the visualization strategy by using the property graph approach, as you will see below.*

The Solution Data Model is created as a derived subset of the business concept model. After that, it is refined and amended.

Requirement 21: **The solution data model is effectively derived from the business concept model.**

This means that some concepts become logical business objects, whereas other concepts become properties of those business objects.

Requirement 22: **The subset of the business concept model is gradually and iteratively extended with design decisions.**

Requirement 23: **It should be easy to establish the lineage from a design object to the business concept model.**

The design decisions will typically enable specific, desired behaviors and solution oriented data.

Requirement 24: The solution model must be visual; the structures being visualized should resemble the structure of the business concept model.

This requirement actually follows from the derivation approach to solution modeling.

Requirement 25: Uniqueness constraints should be defined.

Requirement 26: Since identity is closely related to uniqueness, support for that should also be present.

Requirement 27: There should be support for identifiers, including surrogates.

Requirement 28: There will also be technical and auditing data specified as well as data designed to handle time aspects, such as time series data.

Requirement 29: Cardinalities will be defined on all relationships.

The following meta concepts should be supported:

Requirement 30: Business objects (concepts, which may be referenced from other concepts, and which have properties).

Requirement 31: Properties of business objects (properties are concepts, which share the identity of the business object that owns them).

Requirement 32: Named, directed relationships with precise cardinalities.

Requirement 33: Simple types (e.g. number, string, date, amount).

Today there are a number of physical models available, including:

- Graphs and triple stores
- Key-value stores
- Columnar and BigTable descendants
- Tables (like in relational and SQL methods).

The tabular (relational) model is just one of several. "Decomposition" of the tabular structures (the process known as normalization) is quite complex; it can end up being ambiguous if the semantics are not well defined.

On the other hand, mapping to a tabular result structure from other representations is rather easy—almost mechanical. This means that the tabular model is not a good starting point for a data model, but it might well be a good choice for an implementation model.

What is the good starting point, then? There are some contenders. On the conceptual level, people tend to fall into two camps:

- Those who prefer a business-facing, intuitively simple representation (as is the case with concept maps)

- Those who prefer absolutely tight control over semantics which can be found in various "modeling languages" such as:
    o OWL (the Web Ontology Language from the World Wide Web Consortium)
    o UML (Unified Modeling Language from the Object Management Group)
    o Concept Models are now part of the Object Management Groups (OMG) Semantics of Business Vocabulary and Business Rules (SBVR) standard; which is now adopted by the Institute for Business Analysis, IIBA, in their Business Analysis Body of Knowledge (BABOK) standard
    o ORM (Object Role Modeling supported by the ORM Foundation); a form of Fact Modeling.

Although different, these methods achieve very similar things, and they embed a palette of constructs in support of logic. Logic is necessary because much of computing is about predicate logic. However, logic makes things complex.

When it comes to logic, two of the most difficult decisions that must be made are:

- When to stop modeling data?
- When to start specifying business rules?

I am in favor of simple solutions. Of the four modeling languages mentioned above, the SBVR style concept models are comparable in simplicity to concept maps. Since I also want a data model solution level representation which is simple, communicative, and intuitive, I do not want to include business rules visualization at that level.

Concept maps, of which I am a great fan, are based on directed graphs. So are the semantic technology stacks (W3C's RDF and so forth). Directed graphs seem to be a very good fit for communication structure. We will take advantage of that. The solution data model that we will work with in the remainder of this book is the Property Graph Model. It can look like this:

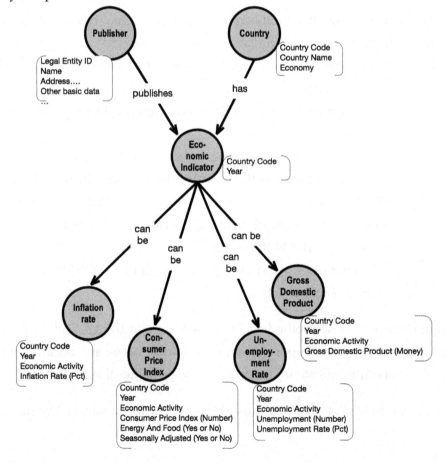

Requirement 34: **Since directed graphs are behind most other data models as an inherent structure, the property graph data model is the chosen paradigm for representing solution data models.**

It is important that the proposed relations between business objects be chosen such that they are (left to right) functionally complete and correct. This behavior was formerly known as normalization.

This concludes the requirements for the solution- (logical-) level data modeling process, and it prepares us for the transition to the physical data model.

3.4.4. ON USING PROPERTY GRAPHS

What graph databases do very well is represent connected data. And as you have seen throughout this book, representing real-world is about communicating these two perspectives:

- Structure (connectedness)
- Meaning (definitions).

Together they explain the context very well. Nodes represent entity types, which I prefer to call types of business objects. Edges, better known as relationships, represent the connectedness and, because of their names, bring semantic clarity and context to the nodes. Concept maps exploit the experiences from educational psychology to speed up learning in the business analysis phase.

That is why the labeled property graph model is the best general-purpose data model paradigm that we have today. Expressed as a property graph, the metamodel of property graphs used for solution data modeling looks like the model on the following page.

The important things are the names and the structures (the nodes and the edges). The properties supplement the solution structure by way of adding content. Properties are basically just names, but they also can signify "identity" (the general idea of a key on the data model level). Identities are shown in italics (or some other stylization of your choice).

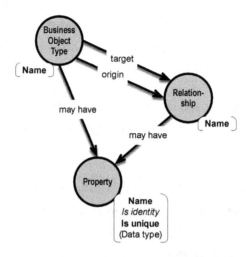

Physical uniqueness is essentially the combination of identities of the nodes included in the path leading to the node whose identity you are interested in. If uniqueness is not established in this intuitive way, you should consider remodeling or documenting the uniqueness in some special fashion. Business level uniqueness is controlled by composite business keys (marked in bold in the property list).

Data types may be added at this stage, but normally they only become important as you get into designing a physical data model. In the NoSQL area you have many more options, including packing things together into long strings or aggregates, as the situation dictates.

3.4.5. PHYSICAL DATA MODEL REQUIREMENTS

It should be easy to implement controlled data redundancy and indexing structures. The physical data model is, of course, dependent on the data store / DBMS of your choice.

Depending on the paradigm of the target system, you will have to make some necessary transformations. However, the solution data model is rather easy to transform into almost anything in a rather mechanical way.

Here are some examples of targets:

- Property graph
- RDF graph
- SQL table
- Key-values and column family store
- Document database.

Requirement 35: **It should be relatively easy to establish the lineage from the physical model to the solution data model, and further on to the business concept model.**

This is best done on top of the solution data model. In fact, in most cases it's as easy as "lassoing" selected parts of the solution data model together, transforming them into aggregates, collections, tables, or any other abstractions necessary. More about that later. A denormalized structure could look like this:

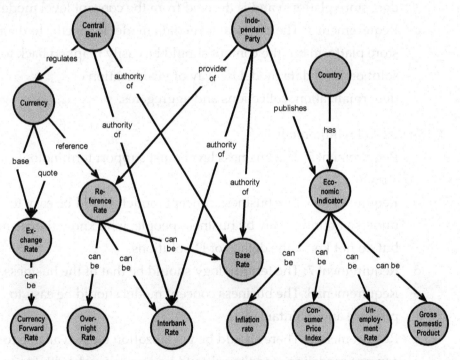

The physical model will contain extensions to the solution data model in the form of performance oriented data, and structures for sorting, searching, and browsing in particular orders.

There will be physical constraints, such as unique indexes, as much as your data store permits. More about this later.

3.4.6. KEEPING IT SIMPLE

In all that we do, we should try to keep things simple. What follows, then, is a complete list of the non-functional requirements for a robust contemporary data modeling "system," as we identified above, for your convenience.

- General requirements
  - Requirement 1: A three level data model architecture.
  - Requirement 2: The business facing level must be built on the concept model paradigm (for visualization and effective learning).
  - Requirement 3: The solution level data model is independent of data store platform and is derived from the concept level model.
  - Requirement 4: The physical level data model is specific to data store platform but the content should be easily mapped back to the solution level data model by way of visualization of denormalization, collections and aggregates.

- Business level requirements
  - Requirement 5: The business level must support terminology and structure.
  - Requirement 6: The business concept model should be easy to understand intuitively by business people, who know the business, but do not know the details of IT solutions.
  - Requirement 7: The terminology should be that of the business.
  - Requirement 8: The business concept model should be easy to produce and maintain.
  - Requirement 9: There should be visualization tools available for concept modeling, and they should be easy to work with for business people.
  - (Optional) Requirement 10: Automated elicitation procedures may be employed (such as text mining and machine learning).

- o Requirement 11: Business Objects.
- o Requirement 12: Properties of business objects.
- o Requirement 13: Atomic values (for illustration purposes).
- o Requirement 14: Named, directed relationships with simple cardinalities.
- o Requirement 15: Directed style for relationships between business objects.
- o Requirement 16: Undirected style for relationships between a business object and its properties.
- o Requirement 17: Generic data types (e.g. number, string, date, amount).
- o Requirement 18: Definitions of the terminology used (word lists with explanations and examples).
- o Requirement 19: Simple business rules written as text.
- o Requirement 20: The Business Concept Models should be approved by the business people, including the sponsors.

- • Solution level requirements
  - o Requirement 21: The solution model is effectively derived from the business concept model.
  - o Requirement 22: The subset of the business concept model is gradually (iteratively) extended with design decisions.
  - o Requirement 23: It should be easy to establish the lineage from a design object to the business concept model.
  - o Requirement 24: The solution model must be visual and the structures being visualized should resemble the structure of the business concept model.
  - o Requirement 25: Uniqueness constraints should be defined.
  - o Requirement 26: Since identity is closely related to uniqueness, support for that should also be present.
  - o Requirement 27: There should be support for identifiers, including surrogates.

- o   Requirement 28: There will also be technical and auditing data specified as well as data designed to handle time aspects, such as time series data.
- o   Requirement 29: Cardinalities will be defined on all relationships.
- o   Requirement 30: Business objects (concepts, which may be referenced from other concepts, and which have properties).
- o   Requirement 31: Properties of business objects (properties are concepts, which share the identity of the business object that owns them).
- o   Requirement 32: Named, directed relationships with precise cardinalities.
- o   Requirement 33: Simple types (number, string, date, amount...).
- o   Requirement 34: Since directed graphs are behind all other data models as the inherent structure, as well as for the business semantics, the property graph data model is the chosen paradigm for representing solution data models.

- Physical level requirement
  - o   Requirement 35: It should be relatively easy to establish the lineage from the physical model to the solution data model, and further on to the business concept model.

This is the result of trying to keep the list as concise as possible, while still scoping a solution that does the job with higher quality and speed than legacy approaches.

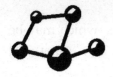

Chapter 4
Data Modeling Described

4.1. SOLUTION MODELING (SOLUTION MODEL)

4.1.1. BUSINESS CONCEPT MODEL

An overview of Business Concept Modeling was covered in Chapter 3. Now we'll focus on the solution modeling activities:

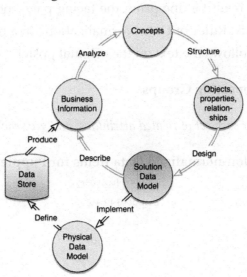

4.1.2. POWER OF DEPENDENCIES

We cannot discuss data modeling without talking about normalization and functional dependencies. We already illustrated the mechanics of the process of normalization in chapter 2. The objectives of eliminating malformed relational data designs are (roughly) these:

- Reduce redundancy
- Avoid update anomalies
- Avoid information loss.

Working around these problems naturally leads to designing keys, which may be primary or foreign. But do we really need normalization and functional dependencies?

To get a feel for the approach that one could call "Relational Data Modeling Classic," let us quickly review orthodox normalization by way of a famous example. This example appeared as a complimentary poster in the Database Programming & Design Magazine published by Miller Freeman back in 1989. The intellectual rights belong to Marc Rettig, now of Fit Associates. It is included here with his kind permission.

Although you cannot read the fine print, the facing page contains the poster in its entirety. Here are the 5 "Rules of Data Normalization" in a more readable fashion. The text here closely follows the text on the original poster.

RULE 1: Eliminate Repeating Groups

Make a separate table for each set of related attributes, and give each table a primary key.

Non-normalized Data Items for Puppies:

Puppy Number
Puppy Name
Kennel Code
Kennel Name
Kennel Location
Trick ID 1..n
Trick Name 1..n
Trick Where Learned 1..n
Skill Level 1..n

In the original list of data, each puppy's description is followed by a list of tricks the puppy has learned. Some might know ten tricks, some might not know any. To answer the question, "Can Fifi roll over?" we need to first find Fifi's puppy record, then scan the list of tricks at the end of that record. This is awkward, inefficient, and untidy.

Moving the tricks into a separate table helps considerably:

Puppy Table	Trick Table
Puppy Number Puppy Name Kennel Code Kennel Name Kennel Location	*Puppy Number* *Trick ID* Trick Name Trick Where Learned Skill Level

Separating the repeating groups of tricks from the puppy information results in first normal form. The puppy number in the trick table matches the primary key in the puppy table, providing the relationship between the two.

RULE 2: Eliminate Redundant Data

"In anything at all, perfection is finally attained not when there is no longer anything to add, but when there is no longer anything to take away."

Saint-Exupéry, *Wind, Sand and Stars*

If an attribute depends on only a part of a multi-valued key, move it to a separate table.

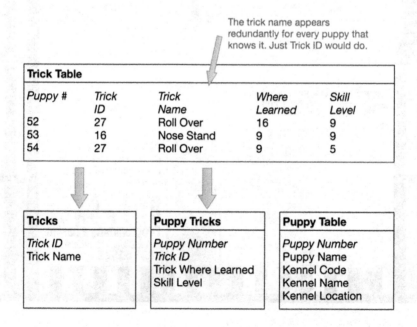

The trick name appears redundantly for every puppy that knows it. Just Trick ID would do.

Puppy #	Trick ID	Trick Name	Where Learned	Skill Level
52	27	Roll Over	16	9
53	16	Nose Stand	9	9
54	27	Roll Over	9	5

Tricks	Puppy Tricks	Puppy Table
Trick ID Trick Name	*Puppy Number* *Trick ID* Trick Where Learned Skill Level	*Puppy Number* Puppy Name Kennel Code Kennel Name Kennel Location

Second normal form

In the Trick Table in the first normal form, the primary key is made up of the puppy number and the trick ID. This makes sense for the "where learned" and "skill level" attributes, since they will be different for every puppy/trick combination. But the trick name depends only on the trick ID. The same name will appear redundantly every time its associated ID appears in the Trick Table.

Suppose you want to reclassify a trick—give it a different Trick ID. The change needs to be made for every puppy that knows the trick! If you miss some, you'll have several puppies with the same trick under different IDs. This represents an "update anomaly."

Or suppose the last puppy knowing a particular trick gets eaten by a lion. His records will be removed from the database, and the trick will not be stored anywhere! This is a "delete anomaly." To avoid these problems, we need the second normal form.

To achieve this, separate the attributes that depend on both parts of the key from those depending only on the trick ID. This results in two tables: "Tricks," which gives the name for each trick ID, and "Puppy Tricks," which lists the tricks learned by each puppy.

Now we can reclassify a trick in a single operation: look up the trick ID in the "Tricks" table and change its name. The results will instantly be available throughout the application.

RULE 3: Eliminate Columns Not Dependent on Key

If attributes do not contribute to a description of the key, move them to a separate table.

The Puppy Table satisfies first formal form as it contains no repeating groups. It satisfies second normal form, since it doesn't have a multi-valued key. But the key is puppy number, and the kennel name and kennel location describe only a kennel (not a puppy). To achieve third normal form, they must be moved into a separate table. Since they describe kennels, kennel code becomes the key of the new

"Kennels" table. The motivation for this is the same as for second normal form: we want to avoid update and delete anomalies. For example, suppose no puppies from the Daisy Hill Puppy Farm were currently stored in the database. With the previous design, there would be no record of Daisy Hill's existence!

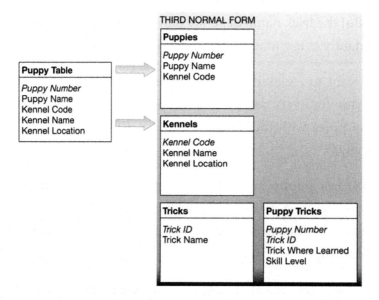

RULE 4: Isolate Independent Multiple Relationships

No table may contain two or more 1:n or n:m relationships that are not directly related.

Rule Four applies only to designs that include one-to-many and many-to-many relationships. An example of one-to-many is that one kennel can hold many puppies. An example of many-to-many is that a puppy can know many tricks, and many puppies might know the same trick.

Suppose we want to add a new attribute to the Puppy Trick table: "Costume." This way we can look for puppies that can both "sit up and beg" and wear a Groucho Marx mask, for example. Fourth normal form dictates against using the Puppy Trick table because the two attributes do not share a meaningful relationship. A puppy may be able to walk upright, and it may be able to wear a suit. This doesn't mean it can do both at the same time. How will you represent this if you store both attributes in the same table?

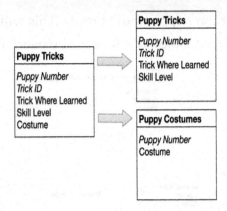

RULE 5: Isolate Semantically Related Multiple Relationships

There may be practical constraints on information that justify separating logically related many-to-many relationships.

Usually, related attributes belong together. For example, if we really wanted to record which tricks every puppy could do in costume, we would want to keep the costume attribute in the Puppy Trick table. But there are times when special characteristics of the data make it more efficient to separate even logically related attributes.

Imagine that we now want to keep track of dog breeds and breeders. Our database will record which breeds are available in each kennel. And we want to record which breeder supplies dogs to those kennels. This suggests a Kennel-Breeder-Breed table which satisfies fourth normal form. As long as any kennel can supply any breed from any breeder, this works fine.

Now suppose a law is passed to prevent excessive arrangements: a kennel selling any breed must offer that breed from all breeders it deals with. In other words, if Kabul Kennels sells Afghans and wants to sell any Daisy Hill puppies, it must sell Daisy Hill Afghans.

The need for a fifth normal form becomes clear when we consider inserts and deletes. Suppose a kennel decides to offer three new breeds: Spaniels, Dachshunds, and West Indian Banana-Biters. Suppose further that it already deals with three breeders that can supply those breeds. This will require nine new rows in the Kennel-Breeder-Breed table—one for each breeder/breed combination.

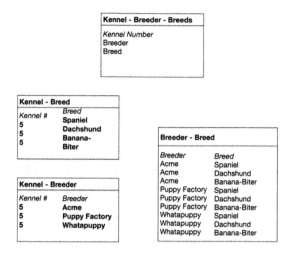

Breaking up the table reduces the number of inserts to six. Above are the tables necessary for fifth normal form, shown with the six newly-inserted rows in bold type. If an application involves significant update activity, fifth normal form can save important resources. Note that these combination tables develop naturally out of entity-relationship analysis.

This is the end of the text from the original poster.

The normalization approach is an example of what happens when one particular scenario is generalized. The assumption being that table design is made from a long list of fields in no particular order. If, on the other hand, the table is based off a structural analysis (like an entity-relationship analysis), there shouldn't be any need to normalize. Instead the structures should be visualized as part of the analysis. You, then, should have no problems deconstructing a graph-based data model (which is what entity-relationship models are all about) into a table-based data model.

Let us turn to the benefits of working with dependencies, staying in the puppy context.

As argued earlier regarding the relational model, things would definitely be easier if the starting point were not a list of fields, but instead a concept map:

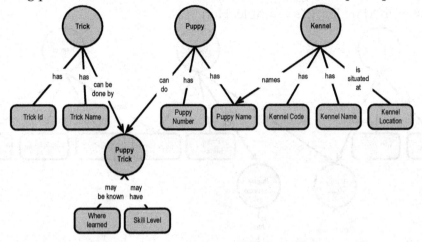

Remember that the way we arrive at a concept map like the above is based on the semantics (meaning) of the linking phrases. Some linking phrases determine a simple dependency (like "has") on the unique identification of the object it is a property of. Other linking phrases contain action verbs meaning that they signify intra-object relationships (like puppy *can do* puppy trick).

So let's work through the process described earlier, from the poster:

Eliminate repeating groups? Not relevant. We already identified them by way of the arrowheads on some of the relationships.

Eliminate redundant data? Not relevant, since a property belongs to one object only, and is identified by its identity.

We will group the properties into tables, if we want to use tables at all. Composition from a well-structured starting point is a whole lot easier than decomposition of a semantically-blurred bunch of data.

Eliminate columns not depending on the key? Not relevant, for the same reason as above.

Isolate independent multiple relationships? Easy. We would add a new object, puppy costume, with a property named costume. We would point at it from the puppy trick, just as in Marc Rettig's example. Here it is:

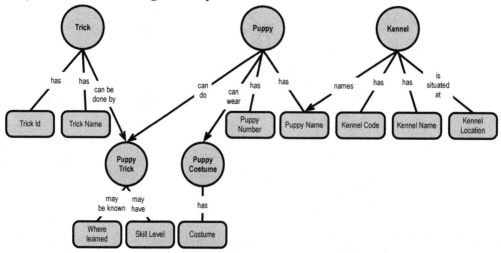

Isolate semantically related multiple relationships? Again, easy. Follow basically the same logic as above. Just as for entity-relationship modeling, as Marc Rettig comments, our concept map or our logical model will naturally show the relationships. Here it is in fifth normal form (5NF):

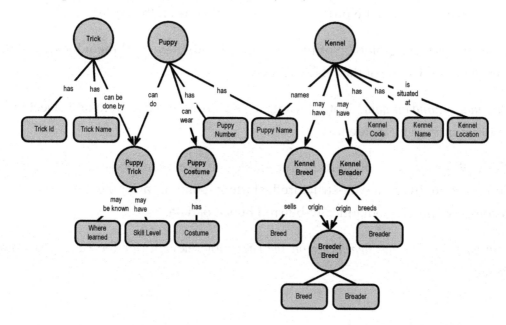

It is obvious that depicting the dependencies as a directed graph gives a deep understanding of the functional dependency structure. There have been only a few attempts at incorporating directed graphs over time:

- Graph Algorithms for Functional Dependency Manipulation by Giorgio Ausiello, Alessandro D'Atri and Domenico Sacca, Journal of the ACM, NO. 10/1983

- The predecessors of the NIAM / ORM Object/Role Modeling paradigm based on Professor Nijssen's work at Control Data in Brussels in the 1980's.

Unfortunately, visual dependency analysis never took off in the 1980's. This was most likely due to the mathematical twist inherent in traditional normalization. Most people were busy implementing SQL and data models soon reflected that the universe of discourse was set to be tables and foreign keys for many years. Only the NIAM / ORM practitioners carried on using their highly visual approach to modeling.

Given that graph visualization is the way forward (as argued so far in this book), is there anything we can carry forward from normalization?

The answer is simple: identity and uniqueness. These two things contribute hugely to setting the context in precise ways. We will come back to this in the section about identifiers, keys, and pointers.

If winding up with a relational data model in the end is not a requirement, you experience more freedom to direct your model design more toward the semantics and reality of business. Do not produce a relational model, if relational is not a requirement.

Aside: Many of the troubles in relational models could have been avoided, if SQL had contained support for dependencies. Let us see, what that could have looked like.

Think of the classic table, Order_Details, as it could be defined in SQL:

```
CREATE TABLE Order_Details (
    OrderID number NOT NULL,
    ProductID number NOT NULL,
    UnitPrice number NOT NULL,
    Quantity number NOT NULL,
    Discount number NOT NULL,
    CONSTRAINT PK_Order_Details PRIMARY KEY
    (
      OrderID,
      ProductID
    ),
    CONSTRAINT FK_Order_Details_Orders FOREIGN KEY
    (
      OrderID
    ) REFERENCES Orders (
      OrderID
    ),
    CONSTRAINT FK_Order_Details_Products FOREIGN KEY
    (
      ProductID
    ) REFERENCES Products (
      ProductID
    )
);
```

Imagine for a few moments that the fathers of relational and SQL got carried away and "materialized" dependencies in more explicit ways:

```
CREATE TABLE Order_Details (
    FOREIGN KEY OrderID NOT OPTIONAL
      DEPENDENCY Order_consists_of
      REFERENCES Orders (OrderID),
    FOREIGN KEY ProductID NOT OPTIONAL
      DEPENDENCY Products_ordered
      REFERENCES Products (ProductID),
    PRIMARY KEY PK_Order_Details
      (OrderID,
      ProductID),
    PROPERTY UnitPrice number NOT OPTIONAL DEPENDENCY has_Price,
    PROPERTY Quantity number NOT OPTIONAL DEPENDENCY has_Quantity,
    PROPERTY Discount number NOT OPTIONAL DEPENDENCY Discount_given,
);
```

Except for the primary key (identity and uniqueness constraint, really), it's all dependencies of either the relationship type or the functional dependency (or primary key) type. Clearly this is much more informative than the relational offering.

End of aside.

Another little aside: Actually dimensional modeling is more interesting than ever. There are definitely good reasons to think in terms of dimensions and facts (or "events"). The granularity of dimensions sets the context of the event. And context is another way of saying "multidimensional coordinates," or "landmarks," in the information "landscape." Event-driven modeling is a very productive way to look at how best to describe business processes.

But first, some practical pieces of advice for preparing a solution data model based on user stories expressed as concept maps.

4.1.3. NAMES MATTER

The transition from concept map to solution data model is somewhat mechanical, as you will see below. Before we get into that, though, we need to reemphasize some things.

Since in some cases the physical data models may be schema-less or schema-on-read, we need a layer of presentation for the business users. That layer is our solution data model.

Furthermore, much of the big data that people want to analyze is more or less machine-generated or system-generated. Again, this calls for a user-facing data layer toward the analytics environment.

Finally, even in integration projects (including most of data warehousing and business analytics), consensus on business names is what is needed to obtain acceptance in the business user community. Names include object type names, property names and relationship names ("linking phrases," in concept-speak).

Relationship names are important because they also are used to infer the type of the relationship (or dependency). Action verbs indicate activity on business objects, whereas passive verbs (like "has") indicate ordinary functional dependencies between an identifier of a business object type and its properties.

Relationships are bidirectional, since they can be read in two ways:

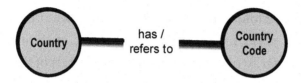

For those reasons, names matter. However, I tend only to write the name coming from the "parent." That would be "has" in this case, since the relationship is one-to-one and left-to-right ordering is applied. The key point is that some linking phrases (the names of relationships, in concept mapping terminology) contain verbs, which imply that somebody or something "makes something happen." In other words, the relationship denotes something which is more than a plain property depending on the identity of something. This makes the target a candidate for being identified as a business object type.

Concepts should also be backed up by solid definitions wherever there is risk of ambiguity. Definitions of core business concepts often persist for a long time and reach many people. This means that they should not only be precise and concise, but they should also be easily communicated and easily remembered. In many respects, production of good definitions is a skill that requires concentration and attention. For world class expertise on good definitions, read this excellent book: "Definitions in Information Management" (Chisholm 2010).

Names should be as specific as they can get. Avoid "Address," if what you are talking about is "Delivery Address." It's always a good idea to consult with a subject area expert to make sure names make sense and are consistent with the business' terminology, before proceeding with the model.

4.1.4. FINDING PATTERNS

Another thing to consider before materializing the solution data model is patterns. Many kinds of business activities and business objects have been defined as best practice data models. It is worth reading David Hay's fine collection of data models in his book, *Enterprise Model Patterns*, Technics Publications (May 15, 2011) [8].

Looking at the last version of the Puppy Kennel concept map, we realize that we need a pattern:

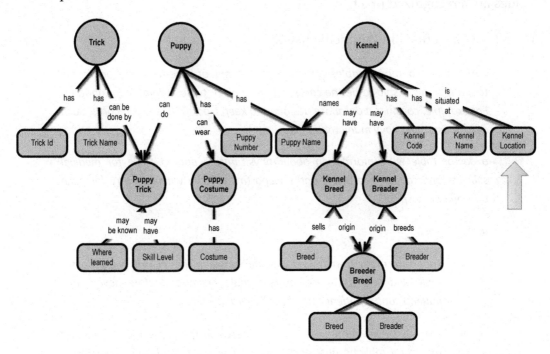

The kennel location property seems a bit un-modeled, if you ask me. Well, Kennels have business addresses, and David Hay has several pages about addresses and geography in his data model patterns book [8].

How did we notice that something was missing about Kennel Locations? Because the linking phrase contains an action verb (situate). Action verbs tend to denote relationships between two object types, not between objects and their properties.

So, that will be another item to check on before transforming to a solution data model.

4.1.5. CARDINALITY AND OPTIONALITY

It can be argued that the issues of cardinality and optionality are coupled to the physical data store (at least in the sense of representation of missing matches). In SQL, this is the crux of the good old "NULL-debate." I tend to stay away from using NULLs. I spend most of my time in data warehouse models, where default values are a recognized practice.

Cardinality is defined in Wikipedia like this:

> In the relational model, tables can be related as any of "one-to-many" or "many-to-many". This is said to be the cardinality of a given table in relation to another. For example, consider a database designed to keep track of hospital records. Such a database could have many tables like:
>
> a doctor table with information about physicians; a patient table for medical subjects undergoing treatment; and a department table with an entry for each division of a hospital.
>
> In that model:
>
> - There is a many-to-many relationship between the records in the doctor table and records in the patient table because doctors have many patients, and a patient could have several doctors;
>
> - There is a one-to-many relationship between the department table and the doctor table because each doctor may work for only one department, but one department could have many doctors.
>
> - A "one-to-one" relationship is mostly used to split a table in two in order to provide information concisely and make it more understandable. In the hospital example, such a relationship could be used to keep apart doctors' own unique professional information from administrative details.

https://en.wikipedia.org/wiki/Cardinality_(data_modeling)

For cardinality, it is good to know whether a relationship is:

- One-to-one or zero/one to zero/one (1:1)
- Zero/one to zero/many (1:M)
- Zero/many to zero/many (M:M).

The 1:1 relationships can be visualized as connections without arrowheads:

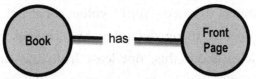

The 1:M relationships can be visualized as a connection with one arrowhead:

The M:M relationships can be visualized as a connection with an arrowhead on both sides.

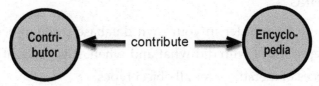

I do not recommend visualizing the starting or ending point as being capable of being "empty." This is, in essence, more related to optionality, which varies across data stores. The matter of optionality is close to being a business rule, which I generally prefer to treat as a layer on top of the data model.

I do recommend that a document be created (and kept up to date) to contain the business-level rules (for things such as optionality and default values), where applicable.

At the physical modeling level, these cardinality issues should, of course, be resolved in a way that matches the capabilities of the platform.

"Optionality" is concerned with the "zero" cases in the cardinalities listed above. Consider 1:M:

- What happens if there is nothing on the "1" side? A doctor not being placed in any department, currently, for example, or
- What happens if there is nothing on the "M" side? A department without doctors, for example.

In SQL there is a much debated "null" value construct. A "null" represents "nothing here". I do prefer using default value schemes over using SQL-nulls. There are many articles about this, not least from the Kimball Group. Topics include:

- Keeping "dummy" records available and letting them participate in hierarchies, etc. (It can be useful to report numbers on "unknown" levels.)
- Using at least an "Unknown" or "Not specified" approach for missing information (if in SQL).
- Using default low and high dates for missing dates.

4.1.6. HOUSEKEEPING

It's best practice to keep order in your own database through accountability. It's important to keep track of who did what and when. It is prudent to keep track of at least these pieces of metadata, for all object types:

- Who created this record?
- When was the record created?
- Who most recently changed this record?
- When was the date and time of the most recent change?

If you are in a data warehouse context (or other data integration contexts), you might also like to include technical metadata about the ETL processes, including:

- Which process loaded this record?
- When was the record loaded?
- What was the source system of the record?
- Versioning control dates (from and to).

4.1.7. MODELING THE SUBJECT AREA OVERVIEW

You'll frequently create a high-level concept map to provide an overview of a subject area. This one is for a car dealership, drawn from my first book [5]:

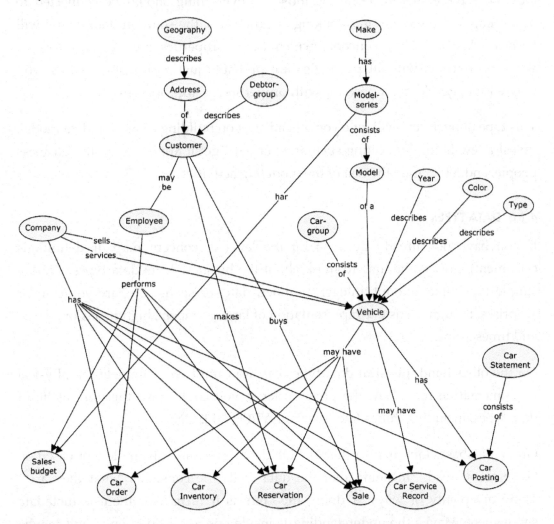

Notice how the upper levels are mostly classifications and other hierarchies. The levels in the middle are the core business objects engaged in the business processes. The concepts at the lowest level are all business events or other records, some of them of the "snapshot" type (like inventory on a given date). Also note that the concepts on the lowest level are actually the "value chain" of the business, starting with budget, flowing over procurement to inventory and sales, and later, maintenance and profitability.

Obviously there should be no "islands," as everything should be connected to something. Once you get into looking at properties, the solution data model will become clearly visible; concepts which carry properties are business objects, whereas concepts without properties are probably just abstractions (which you may wish to get rid of, or describe with properties, as appropriate).

This type of overview will give you a head start on building a solution data model. Invest a few hours in creating such an overview, get it approved by the business people, and let it guide the rest of the modeling activities.

4.1.8. DATA TYPES

If you have not already done so (at the level of concept map or definitions document), now is the time to think about the business level data types. Choose simple types like amount, integer, number, date, or string. Prepare yourself for surprises, though. Consider representation of large numbers, high precision, dates, and timestamps.

On the other hand, physical data types can wait until you complete the physical implementation model. At the physical level, you could have the full palette of data types, including things like Apache AVRO and JSON.

Graph databases (and many other NoSQL data stores) are schema-less or based on "schema on read," meaning that the data "tells the consumer what they are". There are plenty of ways of doing this, but as it turns out, there is metadata somewhere. Maybe the understanding is inside one application only, and maybe there is a metadata catalog in the system. Whichever way, you run into, a structure model of the data as it gives meaning to the business is indeed still necessary.

The real world is kind of messy and half-structured anyway. Forcing that reality into a relational schema, which is hard to maintain, is not the best idea. In relational solutions, that means lots of sparse tables (empty fields) and the infamous complexity of null-handling. That can be avoided in some of the newer technologies, at the expense of higher read-time processing complexity.

4.1.9. IDENTIFIERS, KEYS, AND POINTERS

The days of analyzing functional dependencies (such as looking for foreign keys) are now behind us. The rationale for relational normalization was not clearly stated from a business perspective, but the benefits were clearly related to identity and uniqueness.

These issues are at the level of the solution model. But why do we need to worry about this? The trouble is that we humans do not really care about uniqueness. What is in a name, anyway? We all know that "James Brown" can refer to a very large number of individuals. The trick is to add context: "Yes, you know, James Brown, the singer and the Godfather of Soul." When uniqueness really matters, context is the definite answer.

The requirement for unique identification is, then, an IT-derived necessity. This gave rise to the "artificial" identifiers (Social Security Number, for example) on the business level and the ID fields on the database level. We, as data modelers, must handle these difficult issues in a consistent manner across:

- Identity
- Uniqueness
- Context.

This reflects the observation that cognition is based on "location" in the meaning of "multi-dimensional coordinates." Uniqueness is based on the very same thing.

The end result is that identity is functionally derived from uniqueness, which sets the context. This is the foundation of the commonly discussed "functional dependencies" in relational modeling, including the whole of normalization, candidate keys, primary and foreign keys and what have you.

The relational discussion started sort of backwards. Much of the discussion about candidate keys is based on the assumption that the problem to be solved is structured as follows:

- Here is a relation (or a relvar, strictly speaking) having these attributes (S#, SNAME, etc.).
- What could possibly be the candidate keys?
- What is the quality (uniqueness, I guess) of those keys?

But that is a very awkward starting point. Why pick that particular permutation, out of all the attributes that could eventually contribute to a "well-formed" (normalized) relation (relvar)?

Why not look at context, which for us visual modelers is "business as usual." Let us try doing just that. We will revisit the Puppy / Kennel example as it existed at step 4 (4NF). Identity is really the scope of properties. If we look at skill level and where learned, we can see their scope:

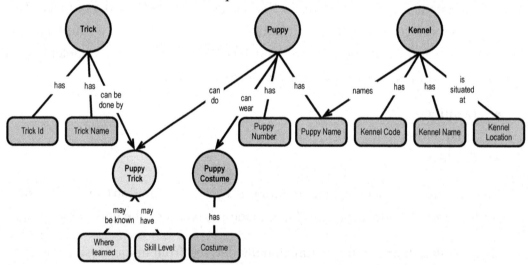

Skill level shares scope with where learned, and both are driven by the identity of the puppy trick. For now, we need to establish a reliable identity of puppy trick. This used to be referred to as "finding the primary key," but I propose we get away the term "keys," since that terminology is closely related to normalization, which is not so relevant anymore.

Uniqueness is the matter of identifying what (on the business level) makes an identity unique. If you are a data modeler, you will not be surprised by the uniqueness behind puppy trick:

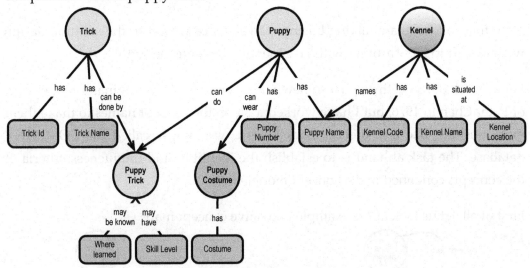

Yes, the puppy trick is uniquely defined by the combination of trick and puppy (i.e. whatever their identities are defined as). Enforcing uniqueness is also an important task in the design of a solution data model. (Previously this was called "foreign keys", but we'll abandon that term too.)

There are no good reasons for adding visual "icons" or special markers, because the uniqueness is implied by the structure. Painting the uniqueness blue wasn't even completely necessary.

Identity determines the scope of a property. Skill level, for example, applies to puppy trick since it is the skill of that Puppy in performing that Trick. Puppy Trick is really a M:M relationship with a few properties attached. The identity of Puppy is simpler, it is the puppy number, which we have designed and introduced with the purpose of representing the identity of the Puppy.

Uniqueness determines the business level criteria for ensuring uniqueness in the database. Puppy trick is unique across the combination of the identities of trick and puppy. Note that uniqueness is always based on the identities and that the representation of the identities may change over time (being redesigned for some reason). In that way, uniqueness is more like a rule, while identity is a representation of something that we use to identify occurrences of business objects in the real world.

Note that so far we are talking business level. Once we get to the solution design we will start to mess around with IT-generated keys and so forth.

Let us work our way through a somewhat larger example. It originates in the work of Peter Chen in 1976, but I have worked a bit on the concept names to make them more business-like and precise. Back then it was simply called the COMPANY database. The task at hand is to establish the identities and uniqueness criteria of the concepts contained in the concept model.

First of all, let us look at the example as a naive concept map:

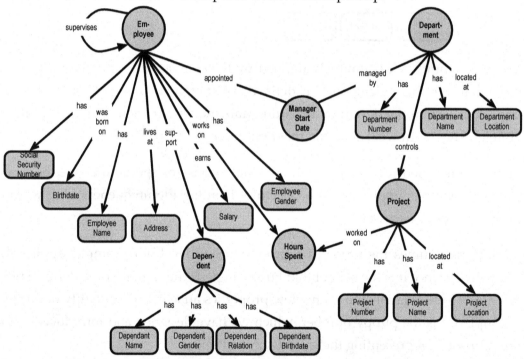

Only one assumption has been made: The manager-related relationship between employee and department is by definition a one-to-one relationship. (And, of course, that departments without managers are not allowed.)

The first step is to check all dependencies (relationships between properties of objects) and identify those properties (remove the arrowheads):

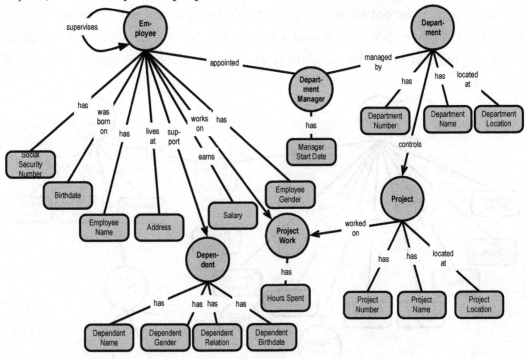

Note that address, department location, and project location very well could have been business object types of some address/geolocation pattern(s). But the data modeler made the business decision that there is no need to keep detailed structures for those fields, since a simple text string will do. This is an example of generalization for simplicity at work.

Also notice that two new concepts have emerged:

- Manager start date is now a property of the new concept of department manager. This change brings clarity and straightforward modeling.

- Hours spent is now a property of the new concept of project work for the same reasons as above.

Finally, the modeler has left the self-reference "supervises" untouched for now.

The next step is to look for natural identities (natural keys / business keys). Before we do that, we'll make another tweak to the example. Using Social Security Numbers (SSNs) are not advisable in Northern Europe (where I am from). For this reason, we'll make SSN an optional alternate key (or search field) and invent an employee number to handle the identity of each employee. This change is reflected here:

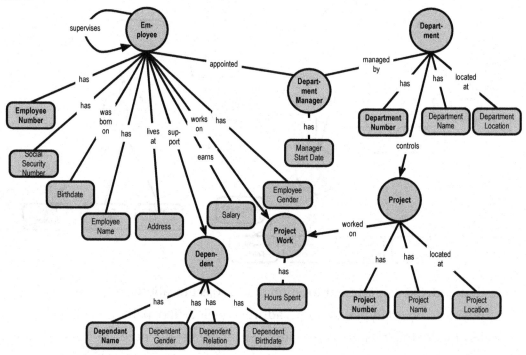

After our slight modification, we can find three natural identity-setting fields (keys, if you insist), and we marked them in bold:

- Employee number (with Social Security Number as an optional alternate)
- Department number
- Project number.

Dependent name is also highlighted, but is has some problems, which we will come back to.

In general, inventing new natural identities can be very practical for us in IT. We have been the ones driving that trend over the years. Business people do not object too much, and at times they can see why such keys are practical.

Dependent really does not have a natural identity. We know that the dependents are depending on an employee, so employee number will be a part of the identity of dependent, but we would like to know more than that. Dependents are clearly "objects" in their own right, by all definitions. It would be tempting to ask for Social Security Numbers, but that is not a path that the business wants to enter. Dependent name is not guaranteed to be unique. We must solve this in our scheme for identity and uniqueness in this model.

Project work and department manager will have composite keys matching the identities of their respective dependency originators. So, we will go forward with the three natural identities we discussed (Employee Number, Department Number, Project Number):

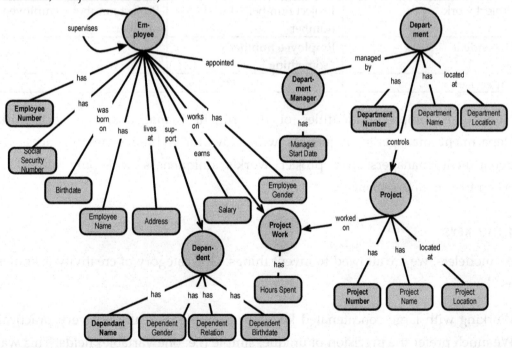

What does this imply for identity and uniqueness? From the diagram above, you can easily see:

- The uniqueness of an object or property is determined by the relationships coming to it from the concepts "higher up"
- The identity of an object is thus the same as the combined identities of the referencing concepts
- Properties, on the other hand, share the identity of the object that they are depending on (which is the defining criterion of a property).

Using these simple "visual inspection" methods, we are able to conclude the context and hence the uniqueness of each object type:

Object type	Identity	Uniqueness
Employee	Employee number	Employee number
Department	Department number	Department number
Project	Project number	Project number
Department manager	Department number + Employee number + Manager start date	Department number + employee number + manager start date
Project work	Project number + Employee number	Project number + employee number
Dependent	Employee number + "something"	?
Supervises?		

Notice the composite identities of department manager and project work. Department manager's uniqueness will allow for a time series of successive department managers. But project work's uniqueness will only allow for accumulating hours spent.

4.1.10. KEYS

As modelers, we are allowed to invent things. One category of creativity is known as "keys."

Working with large concatenated keys, for example, is really not very practical. We much prefer the precision of unique, simple (i.e. one variable) fields. This was first established in 1976, in an object-oriented context. It soon came to rule the world of primary and foreign keys, under the name "surrogate key."

It turned out that business-level keys were rarely single-level fields (unless they were defined by organizers building IT-style solutions). Think account numbers, item numbers, postal codes, and the like. Even if reasonably precise concepts were used, they were not always guaranteed to be unique over a longer period of time. Item numbers, for instance, could be reused over time.

This is why surrogate keys became popular. I have done a lot of modeling in data warehouse contexts and I know from experience how volatile things (even business keys) can be. This is why I recommend always using surrogate keys as a kind of insurance. Non-information-bearing keys are quite practical. Generating them (large integer numbers, for example) is up to the physical platform. But the rule is that the surrogate key should match the uniqueness criteria.

Surrogate keys should be kept inside the database and should not be externalized to business users, but we'll put them into the diagram for now.

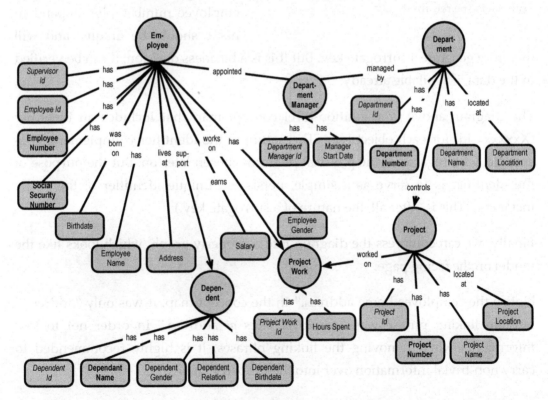

Note how the appearance of physical-level identity insurance (via the surrogate keys) can help us solve the two remaining modeling problems that we had:

> In mainstream data modeling of the last 20-30 years, the use of surrogate keys is not just widespread. Clever people have also given them another purpose: identifying the nonexistent! What many applications nowadays rely on is that Id = 0 (zero, not null) is the representation of the nonexistent instance in the other end of the join. That means, of course, that there should exist a row in the database table referred to in the join, which actually has Id = 0. Those rows typically contain default values for the rest of the fields (properties). The issue here is to avoid the use of SQL outer joins, which would otherwise be required.

"Supervises," which looked a lot like a pointer, can now be implemented as a second surrogate, "supervisor ID," which points to the employee that supervises this employee.

And we can now generate a dependent ID. The business rule for uniqueness could be that the employee number plus dependent name should be unique, and will therefore generate a surrogate key. But this is a business decision; it can be verified in the data, if available already.

The diagram above is a solution-level concept map that includes an identifier (Xxxxxxx Id) for each object type. The nature of the identifier is implementation-specific, with regards to the physical platform chosen later on. But the purpose of the identifier is to serve as a simple, persistent, unique identifier of the object instances. (This is, after all, the nature of a surrogate key.)

Finally, we can compress the diagram into a property graph, which looks like the model on the facing page.

Notice the "employee home address." In the concept map, it was only "address," but the linking phrase was "employee *lives at* address." In order not to lose information when removing the linking phrases, it is highly recommended to carry non-trivial information over into the property names.

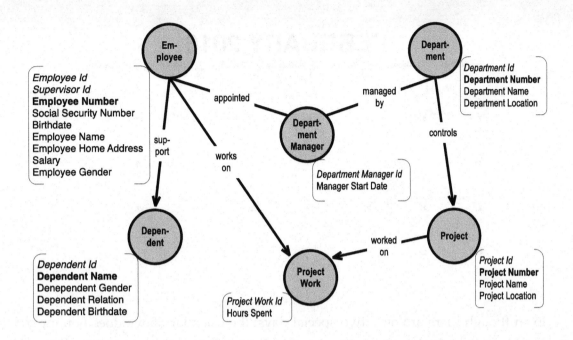

4.1.11. HANDLING TIME

Dates and times are some of the toughest challenges in databases. We have struggled with them since the 1970s. Date and time are mixed into a variety of data types, in many data stores and DBMS products. Some types can be:

- Pure date
- Date and time in one property
- Time in its own property.

Dates and times obey some slightly irregular international rules set for the management of time zones, as you know. They are not systematic in the sense that they can be derived from the value of something. For examples, look up the time zones in and around Australia and the Pacific Islands.

Calendars are somewhat easier, but still subject to a lot of national and cultural variations. Here is a plain US calendar:

FEBRUARY 2016

Sunday	Monday	Tuesday	Wednesday	Thursday	Friday	Saturday
	1	2	3	4	5	6
7	8	9	10	11	12	13
14 Valentine's Day	15 Presidents' Day	16	17	18	19	20
21	22	23	24	25	26	27
28	29					

Powered by www.calendarlabs.com

Even though there are only two special days, the calendar above does not apply outside of the US. Valentine's Day has found its way into Europe, but there is no Presidents' Day. US National holidays are not business days in the US, but they may well be so in other countries. If your data model is required to support global operations, you must cater for this in all date-related logic. You might also need at least four variables on everything:

- Local date (pure)
- Local time (no date involved)
- Global date (pure)
- Global time (set to GMT, for example).

Be mindful of which server you pull the date and time information from. Much depends on the settings of those servers and database instances.

Another issue is the handling of missing dates. If you want to avoid nulls (and who doesn't?), you could define default low and high dates, which are supplied whenever a date (or time of day) is missing. Sometimes we record future dates on records, which are known to us now, but where the event is still to happen within a few years, maybe. The future date could be fixed, like for a date of a dividend payment. But occasionally the future date is not known at this time. This is not very elegant modeling, but it happens in the real world; the consequence is having to define a "future undefined date" (which could also be the general value of a default high date that you have chosen).

On the business level, dates and times serve the purposes of pinpointing the date and time of both events (e.g. sales transactions) and "snapshots" (e.g. inventory counts). A series of transactions is a classic timeline record of events:

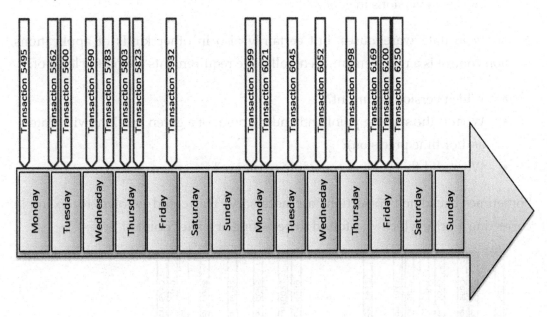

In the data warehousing world, a date/calendar dimension is a given requirement. If your operations are multi-national, you might need several calendars. Just as reporting and analytic applications need to know about calendars (e.g. public holidays, banking days), ordinary applications need to keep track of several properties of dates and times. Prepare accordingly.

Sometimes you have to handle state changes. In the financial world, for example, buy/sell transactions in securities can be in one of several states at any given time. Over time they ascend raised up through a hierarchy states much like this:

- Considered
- Planned
- Agreed

- Preliminarily booked
- Settled
- Finally accounted for.

That means that the same transaction exists in different versions throughout its lifecycle. Date and time are necessary to keep track of these different versions.

This brings us to versions in general.

Not only in data warehouses, but certainly also in other kinds of applications, version control is a requirement. Generally, the requirements are on the level of:

- Which version is current?
- What is the starting point and ending point of a given version (with date and/or time precision)?
- When did this version come into existence?

Sometimes backdated corrections are necessary. This could involve, for example, correcting a price which was found to be wrong at a later point of time:

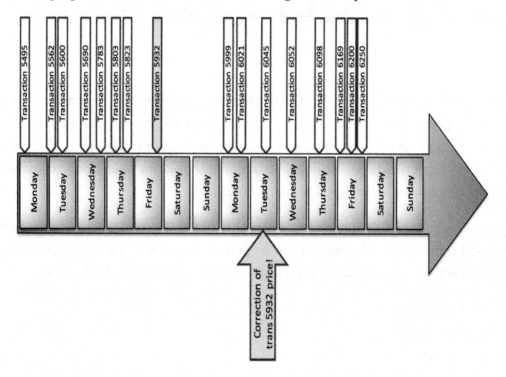

Obviously, keeping two versions depends on accounting practices and possibly also regulatory requirements. Check carefully with someone familiar with business rules and requirements to determine your particular situation.

If you are into versioning, you could consider modeling concepts as chains of events. For instance: "The next event following this version of this transaction is XXXXX on date YYYYMMDD." Graphs are excellent for modeling and implementing these. You might also be interested in prior event chains. For instance: "The event that preceded this version of this transaction was XXXXX on date YYYYMMDD."

4.1.12. DESIGN INVOLVES DECISIONS

Never forget that data modeling is <u>design</u>! Design means making decisions—decisions that impact the business quality of the solution.

If you haven't noticed by now, we often encounter a dilemma between supporting the business, with its processes and questions (both present and future), and keeping things simple. A balanced solution is what we should strive for.

Note that the conceptual model, if you have one, is often very liberal regarding dependencies and other structural issues. You do have to keep an eye on the structure (which is inherent in the data), once you get around to modeling it.

One of your best helpers is a good concept model with meaningful linking phrases (names of dependencies). Remember from earlier that concepts relate to other concepts in a sentence-like (subject - predicate - object) manner, such as "customer places order." As we've discussed, the verbs in those little sentences tell you a lot about the structure. Is the target just a property? "Is" or "has" in the linking phrase will indicate that. Is there a full-blown relationship between business objects? "Places," for example, indicates a process that transforms a state of the business to another state ("ordered", for example).

We do have some generally applicable "designer tools" in our mental tool belt:

- Abstraction, i.e. generalization and specialization, a.k.a. aggregation

- Classification and typing
- Life-cycle dependencies and versioning
- Recognizing hierarchies.

There are also some problem areas to be aware of:
- One-to-one relationships
- Many-to-many relationships and nested object types
- Trees (hierarchies of different kinds).

We'll examine these issues in the following sections.

In general, generalization involves making things more widely usable—expanding the applicable context. But specificity strengthens the comprehension of that particular context.

In chapter 6 we will delve into some of these issues. Here are some helpful tips to get you started:

- Do not force business objects into relationships.
- Be careful with understanding linking phrases (verbs are good indicators of relationships).
- If you're not sure whether something is a property or a relationship, check the verbs!
- Do not use composite values (repeating groups).

Good craftsmanship means that what you build lasts a long time. Think about what the data model can be used for—both now and in the future. Try to make it more widely accessible, but do not generalize it ad absurdum.

Also consider the lifespan of the terminology and concepts used. Will they last long enough? Will they be understood by business users coming on board five or ten years from now?

And remember that design decisions impacts the business. Ensure proper acceptance from those folks, before you force them into something that they find awkward or downright wrong. Acceptance can be a nod of the head or also a formal sign-off event at the other end of the formalism scale.

4.1.13. ABSTRACTION, SPECIALIZATION, AND GENERALIZATION

Abstraction is the strongest problem-solving weapon in your arsenal as a data modeler. Abstraction involves creating layers:

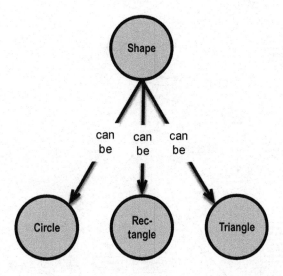

Here you can "generalize" circles, rectangles, and triangles to be shapes. Or you can "specialize" shapes into being circles, rectangles and triangles. Moving up to a higher level layer is generalizing, and specializing involves working your way down into more and more detail.

Generalization generally makes things more broadly useful; at the same time, some details are sacrificed. Specialization, on the other hand, gets you more detail and more complexity. Make sure to consult your business contacts about how much specialization (or lack thereof) they really want and need. Another way of expressing this is with terms like "supertypes," "subtypes," and the like. If you're using that terminology, the question to ask becomes: "Do we want the subtypes to be materialized in the solution model, or not?" One key issue, of course, is what to do with subtype-specific properties.

As background for the discussion, here is a concept model of a subset of FIBO (Financial Industry Business Ontology), which is described further in section 5.4. The conceptual level is carefully modeled and described in the semantic web standards OWL and RDF, so every detail about subtypes and all of the rest are fully documented. I have simplified matters a bit to look like this:

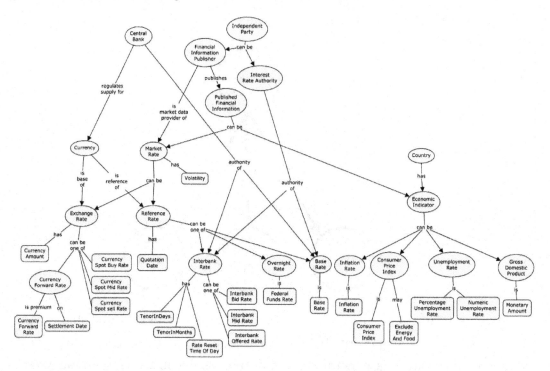

Here we will look at specific issues related to our discussion about abstractions. First of all, there are an abundance of "independent parties" at the top of the concept model:

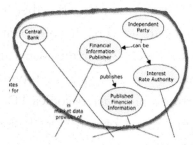

In fact, "central bank" is also a subtype of independent party (of the type monetary authority). All of the parties have very similar attributes, inherited from a "formal organization" supertype. We will therefore generalize them into one type of business object, called "party." This kind of "player / agent" generalization is quite common; it has both advantages and disadvantages. Here we prioritize simplicity so that party gets all of the relationships:

- Regulates (currencies, accomplished by central banks)
- Market data provider
- Publisher
- Authority (either an authorized independent party or a monetary authority).

To keep the information about the important subtypes (which we have eliminated via generalization), we have introduced a couple of categorizations into the solution model at the party level:

- Monetary authority (yes or no)
- Interest rate authority (yes or no).

They are just properties, though, at the party level:

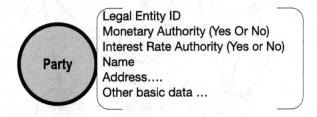

Notice that the concept "Published Financial Information" is really just a categorization of market rate and economic indicator. From a practical point of view, it does not garner a whole lot of information; as such, and it is ignored in the solution data model.

Looking at the full concept model above, you will notice that "market rate" only carries one property: volatility. To maintain it as a separate level seems like overkill, so we will introduce a little bit of redundancy and push it down to the subtypes of market rate. Such "pushing down" is quite common. In our case, it is perfectly acceptable because volatility is dependent on the rate at the given point of time; you will only find this at the lowest level of the rate subtype instances, anyway. The FIBO conceptual model is not really concerned with how to handle time-series data; it focuses mostly on the concept level.

The solution data model will pretty much follow the structure of the concept model, as you can see in a first approximation here:

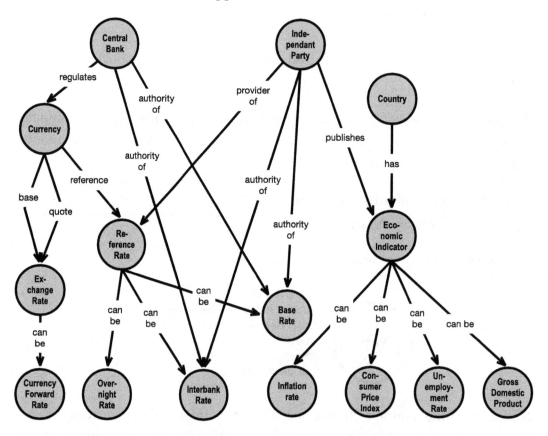

The properties shown in the concept model above will be placed on the lower level (containing rate business object types). More on this in chapter 5.

4.1.14. UNUSUAL CONCEPTS

Sometimes you may run into "unusual concepts," which must be handled in unique ways. One of the scenarios is the "nested object types," a term used in the context of fact modeling. Here is a naive representation of one such example:

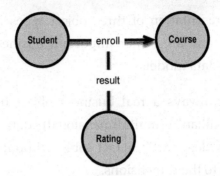

Students enroll in courses, and each enrollment results in a rating. Basically, this is a ternary relationship—there are 3 participating concepts. Notice that the *resulting* relationship is of the arrow-less, one-to-one type; it emerges from the many-to-many relationship between students and courses.

One good way to visualize this is by taking advantage of the property graph model's ability to have properties on relationships:

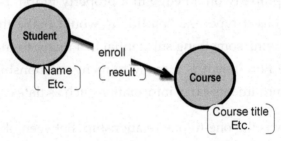

This works well if your final destination is a property graph database (such as Neo4j). However, it your target is a SQL database, you will most likely end up having three business object types:

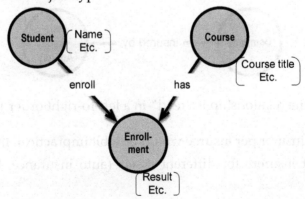

In my opinion, the representation of three object types is fair and to the point. Enrollments do happen and are rather important business events, which makes them emphasized in the data model.

In fact, there is almost always a real business object behind a many-to-many relationship. In "Kimballian" (multidimensional) data modeling, there is a construct called the "factless fact": a fact table without any other information beyond the foreign keys to the dimensions.

Such a table is the "mother of all relationships." In fact (pun intended), even factless facts most often have properties (or measures), once you start looking for them.

Another common use of properties on the relationship level is "weight." This could signify, for instance, participation or part-ownership. This could certainly be implemented as a property on an edge in a property graph, but in most peoples' minds, a business object type like "partition" would make the most sense. This brings us back to having something substantial in a many-to-many relationship: In the example above Enrollment is a many-to-many relationship between Student and Course. And Enrollments carry information such as dates.

Another odd fellow is the one-to-one relationship. Between object types and their properties there are always one-to-one relationships—they're also known as dependencies. But one-to-one's do occasionally arise between business object types. Most instances occur in the realm of business rules. Here is one example:

(Remember that the relationship is "read" in a left-to-right order.)

Having only one insurer per insuree would be a bit impractical. In real life, most of us have different insurers for different assets (auto insurance, health insurance, etc.).

Self-references also crop up in data models from time to time. Here is a simple example that we saw earlier:

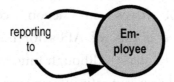

It is worth checking whether the relationship is information-bearing. That could well be the case, like in this example:

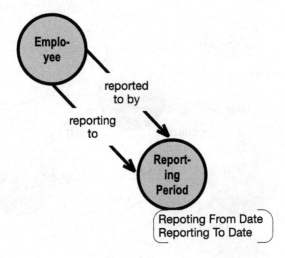

This, by the way, once again confirms the assumption that many-to-many relationships are most often information-bearing constructs.

In general, graphs are very good at representing hierarchies, and the classic balanced tree is easy to model (one node for each level in the hierarchy). In reality, balanced and unbalanced trees require the good old friends of the network databases of the past to help you generalize a graph model.

Nodes are excellent ways to represent the vertices of a tree. In the completely generalized tree, then, you will have a data model with one "multi-purpose" node. You could just call it a "Node", or you could, sometimes, find a more specific name. Consider the variety of relationships (edges) that are available for use:

parent/child, first/last, next/prior, and many more. Using this wide variety of relationship semantics, you can build most kinds of trees.

One good example of trees in action comes from Graphaware (http://bit.ly/2adnn88). It's a library of API's for building time trees in Neo4j, which is a property graph database. Although time hierarchies are balanced, you can benefit from the general tree semantics, as you see in the Graphaware example below:

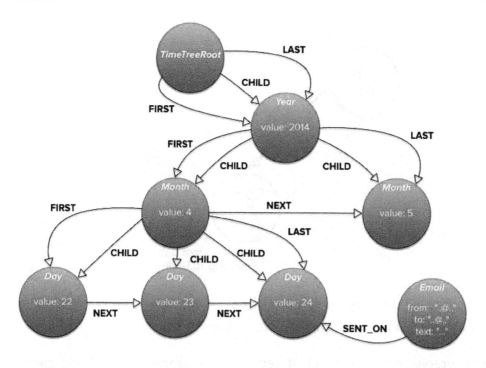

Graphaware is available on a GNU General Public License

If your target is a graph database (or some document database), tree semantics will suit your needs. If you are aiming for a key-value-based implementation, you can also map a tree to such a physical model relatively easily. But if you are targeting a SQL database, you must be brave hearted. You will be using surrogate keys and utilizing multiple pointer fields in your tables.

For advice on modeling tree structures in SQL, consult Joe Celko's *Trees and Hierarchies in SQL for Smarties*.

4.2. TRANSFORM, OPTIMIZE, AND DEPLOY (PHYSICAL MODEL)

4.2.1. CREATING THE PHYSICAL MODELS

It's time to enter the lowest layer of the data modeling zone:

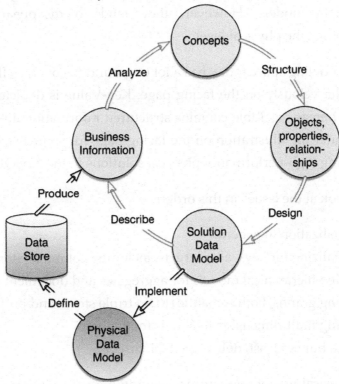

Transforming the solution data model to a concrete physical model is a pleasant task that demands both familiarity with 1) business requirements (user stories) and 2) competency in physical modeling (for the target of your choice).

At this point in the process, you'll likely already be quite familiar with the business requirements at hand; they've been relevant in every step.

This book does not intend to help you with the second requirement. There exist plenty of other good sources, closer to the vendors, which can help you with that.

Here we will examine how our visual representations of concept maps and solution data models can help us determine which transformations we will need.

We'll also get useful mapping information on the business level, if we visualize the selected transformations.

A good example of the synergy between the three modeling levels is the matter of hierarchies. These exist on the business level, and can be seen in concept maps and in solution data models. However, they tend to disappear (because of denormalization) at the physical level.

The physical modeling space today has a lot of ground to cover, as Ilya Katsov has illustrated so marvelously on the facing page. Key-Value is depicted as having a single value, whereas Big Table contains structured information. Refer to the blog post quoted under the illustration on the facing page for some excellent technical advice on making high-performance physical solutions in the NoSQL context.

Here we will look at the issues in this order:

- Denormalization in general
- Denormalizing for key-value targets, including columnar stores
- Delivering hierarchical models for aggregates and document stores
- Delivering graphs, both semantic (RDF) triple stores and property graphs
- Delivering multidimensional models for analytics
- And last, but not least, delivering SQL targets!

The type of physical model you end up using in a given solution can have some effects on requirements for detailed preservation of history (e.g. Type 2 level of versioning as it appears in data warehouses and other places). If you have those kinds of requirements, please make sure your choice of physical data store is compatible with them.

Also remember that most of these products do not "join" in the SQL sense. Document and graph databases do offer good possibilities for relating things; otherwise, you will have to rely on applications to perform joins. This will influence your design; you should try to cater to frequent query patterns in the design of the physical data model. Identifying these is what the user stories are for. Go back to your concept maps and consult the business level relationships/dependencies before you get too deep into the physical design.

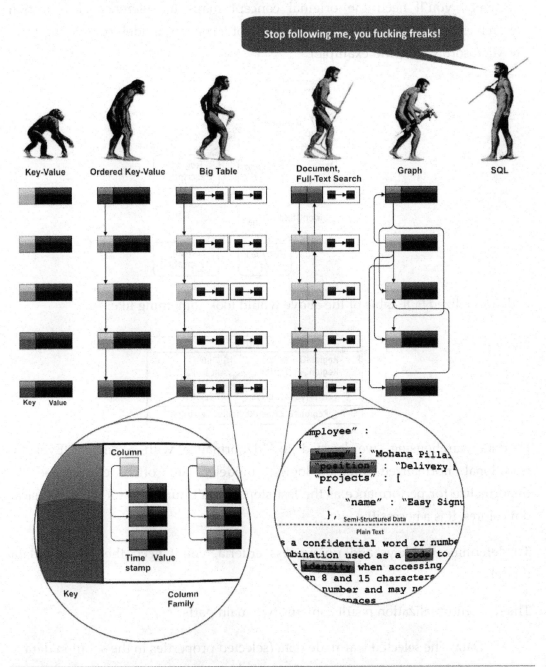

4.2.2. DENORMALIZE WITH A SMILE

Denormalization and duplication are your good friends. To denormalize effectively, you'll need the original concept maps to reference classification hierarchies and the like. Here is an example of a concept model (originating from the Microsoft Northwind example):

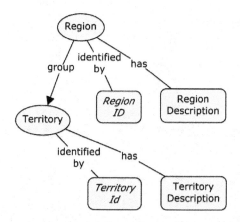

A denormalized SQL table of the above would look something like:

Territory		
P * RegionID	NUMBER	
* RegionDescription	VARCHAR2 (50)	
P * TerritoryID	VARCHAR2 (20)	
* TerritoryDescription	VARCHAR2 (50)	
⌦ PK_RegionTerritory (RegionID, TerritoryID)		

In data warehousing, we learned to "denormalize with a smile"! Even in traditional normalized methodologies, modeler are often encouraged to denormalize for performance as the last step. It can't hurt, and for some physical data stores, it is a necessity.

To determine the keys and uniqueness criteria, you'll need the solution data model.

The flat denormalization result contains two main parts:

- **Data**: The selected leaf-node data (selected properties in the solution data model—in this case, the description fields)

- **Navigation fields**: The intermediate and top-level node properties (including identity keys), and the intermediate levels of classification hierarchies (in this case, the TerritoryID and RegionID).

As you can see from this example, it is important to include all necessary intermediate and top-level keys. Otherwise, you will not be able to uniquely identify each row in the result. This is called "getting the grain right" in star schema modeling; it is absolutely necessary for getting correct aggregated numbers in reports run on top of flat denormalization results.

Denormalization also introduces another basic violation of the normalization principles: the constructs called "repeating groups." We see them all the time, as in this example:

Customer			
Customer ID	**First Name**	**Surname**	**Telephone Number**
123	Robert	Ingram	555-861-2025
			555-403-1659
456	Jane	Wright	555-776-4100
789	Maria	Fernandez	555-808-9633

Source: http://bit.ly/2a2wWVr

Jan Wright has two telephone numbers; this leads to a repeating set of values within the same row. Transforming it to first normal form yields:

Customer			
Customer ID	**First Name**	**Surname**	**Telephone Number**
123	Robert	Ingram	555-861-2025
456	Jane	Wright	555-403-1659
456	Jane	Wright	555-776-4100
789	Maria	Fernandez	555-808-9633

Source: http://bit.ly/2a2wWVr

Obviously, we now have a repeating group of data. However, in data warehousing (and also in NoSQL), this is widely used as a pragmatic solution in various scenarios.

Note that denormalization can be used in different situations:

- Defining key-value structures, possibly containing multiple keys and/or multiple value columns

- Building concatenated data (e.g. JSON) to be used in single-valued key-value stores (also called "wide column stores")

- Building aggregates in the sense used in Domain Driven Design

- Building nested sets for document style structures.

Another option is using repeating groups of columns. If there aren't too many in a 1:M relationship, repeating groups could work well and give you extra retrieval speed.

Refer to the following sections for more information about each of the use cases.

4.2.3. KEY / VALUE TARGETS

Key-value stores differ in their physical model. Key-wise, they contain either just one key or multiple key fields (implying a hierarchical structure of the data). Column-wise, they include either just one value column (which may become very large) or multiple value columns.

These last cases (i.e. those with multiple value columns) are described by many names: "column family databases," "big tables," "wide tables," or "long row designs". Essentially, the column-wise physical models are applications of the repeating group paradigm, such that every row contains column(s) for each occurrence of the repeating data. Consider, for example, the multiple phone number example above (recall section 4.2.2.).

Denormalization will have to cater to that. For example, sketching an aggregate structure (in the domain-driven design paradigm) could look like this:

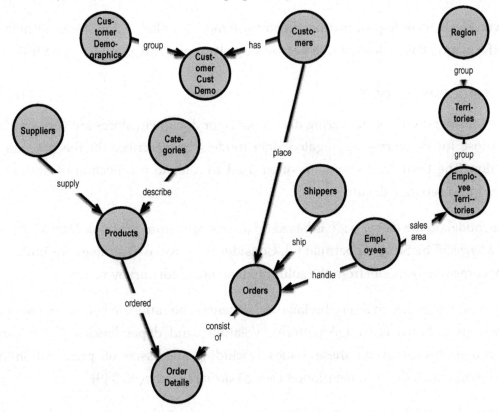

The resulting sets of data can be transformed further (e.g. into JSON or Apache AVRO), but I will leave that to you.

If you use a single-valued key-value approach, you could introduce an extra "navigation field" denoting the type of content in the data column. It can be very simple, such as: "Name: Thomas."

That pattern could extend over multiple levels down a hierarchy: "Person:Employee:Name:Thomas." The recursion could also happen as "materialized paths" of data: "Shoes:Men's shoes:Boots…"

Aggregates essentially deliver hierarchies for each relevant sub-tree of the solution data model. Note that aggregation might imply denormalization as well; the result will always have redundant data. Consider this when designing your model. If the redundant data is processed at different stages of a lifecycle, it might work well.

If you really want to power-tune the physical models of key-value stores for high performance, have a look at Ilya Katsov's excellent blog: http://bit.ly/1zmWIpP.

4.2.4. DOCUMENT STORES

The considerations for delivering data models for document stores are very similar to those for delivering aggregated data models, as described in the preceding section. The term "collections" is often used to refer to a collection of data that goes into a separate document.

The model on the facing page is based on an example from the book *Data Modeling for MongoDB* by Steve Hoberman [9]. Consider this proposed strategy for building a document data model from the solution data model for survey results.

In essence, you design a set of related documents. The rationale behind the design decisions is based on usage patterns, volatility, and dependencies. For a very thorough discussion on these issues (including the issue of preservation of history), consult the aforementioned *Data Modeling for MongoDB* [9].

Many document stores offer flexibility of choice between embedding or referencing. Referencing allows you to avoid redundancy, but at the cost of having to retrieve many documents. In fact, some products go to great lengths to deliver graph-style capabilities, both in the semantic "RDF triplets" style and in the general "directed graph" style.

In this manner, what your physical design will likely end up with is a set of related collections that reference each other; these could be arranged in many-to-many relationships, if need be.

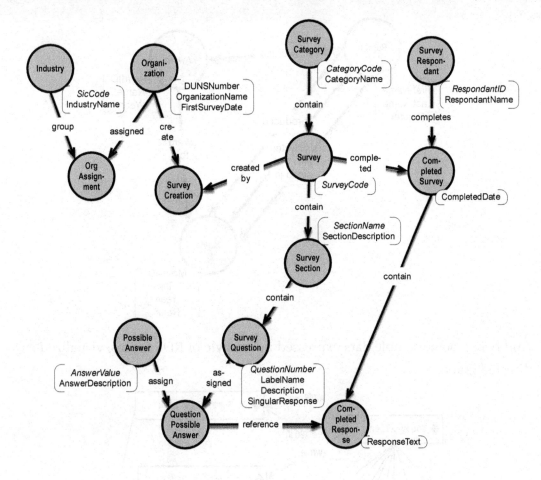

4.2.5. RDF AND TRIPLESTORES

Delivering a triple store solution for a RDF database is rather easy on the structural level. It basically involves a serialization of the concept maps behind the solution data model, supplemented with solution-level keys and properties if necessary.

Here is a simplified solution data model modeled after the Internet Movie Database (www.imdb.com):

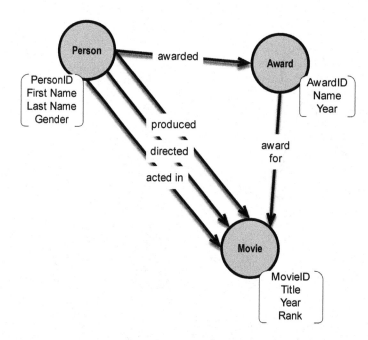

And here is some sample data expressed in the style of RDF triples, visualized as a directed graph:

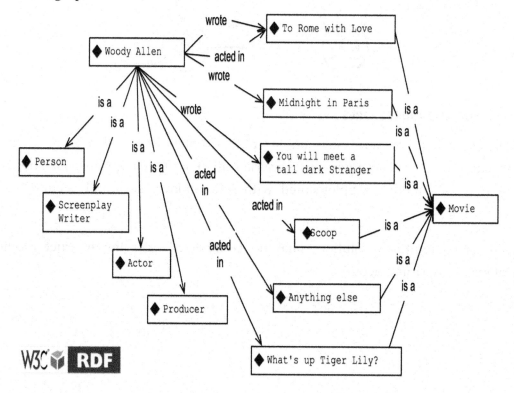

Basic RDF is an XML language that looks like this (in a very simple example):

```
<?xml version="1.0" encoding="UTF-8?">
<!--
   Sample RDF from the PRISM specification - section 2.7.1
   Version 1.0; April 9, 2001
-->
<rdf:RDF xmlns:prism="http://prismstandard.org/1.0#"
      xmlns:rdf="http://www.w3.org/1999/02/22-rdf-syntax-ns#"
      xmlns:dc="http://purl.org/dc/elements/1.1/">
<rdf:Description
      rdf:about="http://wanderlust.com/2000/08/Corfu.jpg">
 <dc:identifier rdf:resource="http://wanderlust.com/content/2357845"
      />
 <dc:description>Photograph taken at 6:00 am on Corfu with two
      models</dc:description>
 <dc:title>Walking on the Beach in Corfu</dc:title>
 <dc:creator>John Peterson</dc:creator>
 <dc:contributor>Sally Smith, lighting</dc:contributor>
 <dc:format>image/jpeg</dc:format>
</rdf:Description>
</rdf:RDF>
```

The example is taken from the publicly available W3C tests library (http://bit.ly/29PoXIs). And don't worry—RDF is meant for machine consumption!

RDF is a schema-description language based on concepts such as classes, sub-classes, properties, sub-properties, types, domains, and more. Transforming a solution data model (expressed as a property graph) to RDF is rather mechanical. You will have to make decisions about whether a concept is best expressed as a class/sub-class or a named relationship. Query-wise, the results are equivalent; it is more a matter of style. On the physical level there can exist several other activities, like defining a RDF Schema describing the metadata of the model, or taking the whole model to the ontology level and expressing it in OWL (Web Ontology Language).

For more information on advanced applications of semantic standards and technologies, consult "Semantic Web for the Working Ontologist," by Dean Allemang and Jim Handler.

4.2.6. PROPERTY GRAPHS

Since our solution data model is already a property graph, moving it to a property graph platform is very easy.

Look at the examples in section 4.1, and later in chapter 5. If you want more "graph-ish" modeling tips, you can look into this (free) book from Neo4j: http://bit.ly/29VFvPZ.

Property graphs are quite rich in their expressiveness, as you have seen already in the solution modeling chapter.

What we did not discuss in depth were properties on relationships, which should be used for describing some important feature(s) of the relationship like strength, weight, proportion, or quality.

Relationships are essentially joins between nodes, with one big difference. A relationship called "produces" may well point to different types of business objects, like "part" and "waste." This is both a strength and a weakness. It's positive because it reflects the way people think about reality. It's negative because people might get confused, if the semantics are unclear. These considerations are very good reasons to define a solution data model, even if your physical data model is going to be based on a "flexible" or even non-existing schema.

Much of the flexibility of the graph model can be used to handle specialization on the fly. That is fine in most cases, but specializations hang off more precisely defined structures. And the precisely defined structures is what you have in your solution data model.

In graph databases you can use ordered, linked lists. Neo4j mentions (in an article) two examples of such lists:

- A "next broadcast" relationship, linking the broadcasts in chronological order

- A "next in production" relationship, ordering the same broadcasts in sequence of production.

Here is an example of establishing purchasing history for customers by way of using a "next order" relationship:

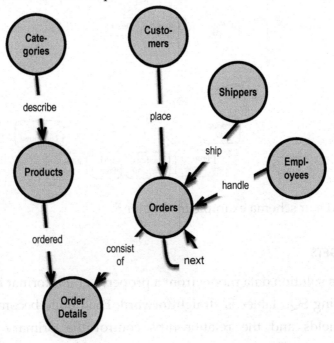

Prior links could also be useful in situations like this. "Prior orders" could be useful in some applications.

In this manner time-series data can be handled elegantly in graphical representations using next / prior linking.

If you find yourself working extensively with these applications that work well with graph databases, you can bite the bullet and go "all graphs." Alternatively, you can architect a solution that is part-graph and part-something else (SQL, for example).

4.2.7. MULTIDIMENSIONAL MODELS

Multidimensional systems are based on table concepts, for the most part. Tables are denormalized. For that reason, you will need to consult the concept models to find detailed information about the hierarchies within the dimensions. Here is an example of a product's dimensions:

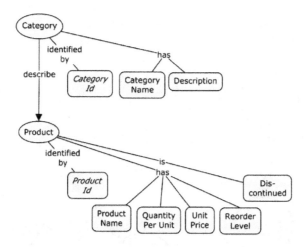

See the detailed star schema example in chapter 5.

4.2.8. SQL TARGETS

Transforming a solution data model from a property graph format into a relational data model using SQL tables is straightforward. Each node becomes a table, and the identity fields and the relationships control the primary / foreign key structures.

In the little employee-department data model from the seventies, the transformations look like this. First, the solution data model:

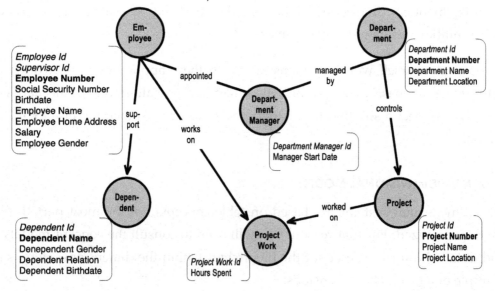

And then, the key structures:

Table	Unique business key	Unique physical primary key	Foreign keys
Employee	Employee number	Employee ID	Supervisor ID
Dependent	Dependent name	Dependent ID	Employee ID
Department manager		Department manager ID	Employee ID, department ID
Project Work	Project number	Project Work ID	Employee ID, project ID
Department	Department number	Department ID	
Project	Project number	Project ID	Department ID

There could be situations where you want to tweak the physical SQL model a bit. Parts of the model might be too low-level or too high-level for the practical purposes of the database. In these cases, you must generalize or specialize. Back to the drawing board.

You might also want to denormalize some parts to get better performance. Remember, though, that the penalty for denormalization is trouble with update. If you denormalize, it is a good idea to look at the lifecycle of the entity types involved, to see if they (in reality) are actually independent of each other. If they are not updated together, it might not be a good idea to denormalize. If you are building analytical solutions, go ahead and build a denormalized, multidimensional physical model.

With that, we'll examine some more involved examples.

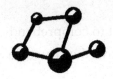

Chapter 5
Selected Detailed Examples

5.1. FROM RELATIONAL MODEL TO PROPERTY GRAPH MODEL

Northwind was one of the sample databases published by Microsoft for SQL Server. It was for use with SQL Server 7 and SQL Server 2000. In 2005 it was replaced by the more comprehensive Adventureworks sample database. Northwind can still be downloaded from Microsoft: http://bit.ly/2a2xtGM. The data model looks like this:

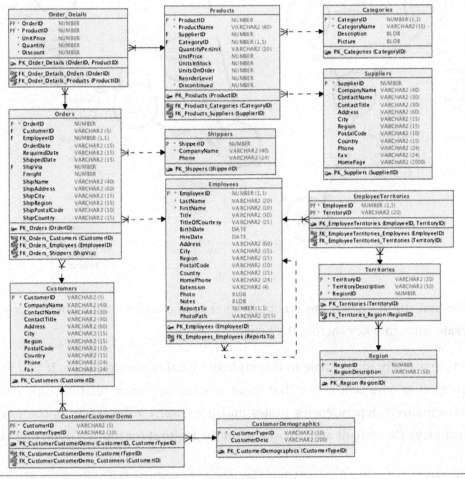

Diagram built by the author in Oracle SQL Developer Data Modeler

Although not truly complex, the one-page diagram is a bit difficult to comprehend without a conscious effort. The presentation style simply underplays the structure of the tables' field lists.

In the property graph style advocated by this book, the solution data model could look like this:

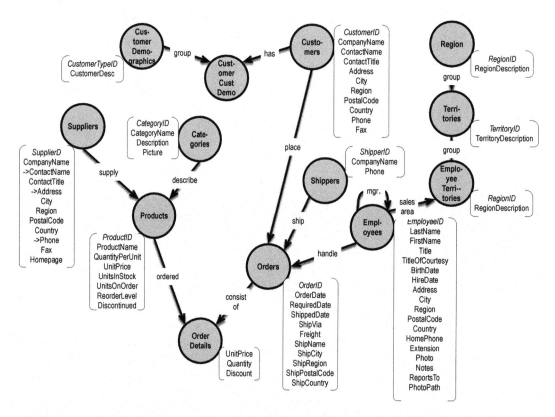

Notice that the ID fields are business level fields, and that we should probably generate surrogate keys across the board.

Structure is easily identifiable in this style of visual communication. If you look at the properties, you will notice that there actually are some relationships reduced to denormalized dependencies (dates and geography roles, such as country and shipcountry). Be vigilant and always be on the lookout for hidden dependencies.

5.2. A MULTIDIMENSIONAL MODEL

Transforming a relational data model into a multidimensional model involves some restructuring of the relationships. Multidimensional data models are sometimes called "star schemas" because they center on a central fact (table) being surrounded by a layer of dimension tables.

For more on multidimensional modeling, read *The Data Warehouse Toolkit: The Definitive Guide to Dimensional Modeling, 3rd Edition* by Ralph Kimball and Margy Ross. Or Google the term – there are plenty of articles out there.

Let us tweak the data model we made in the previous section (inspired by Microsoft's Northwind training data model) into a multidimensional model. First we have to identify the fact tables (business events). There are five candidates:

- Orders
- Purchase orders (with suppliers of products)
- Inventory (of product)
- Customer demographics, and
- Employee territories.

(Multidimensional models typically transform many-to-many relationships into separate fact tables.)

We can now create a first draft of a star schema for the orders fact, as shown on the next page.

Notice how the relationships are now targeting orders directly. This makes sense for two reasons:

- The shippers used to handle orders (which we now call order header) will degenerate in the next steps

- The suppliers do supply products, but that is part of the purchase order context, which we're skipping in this book.

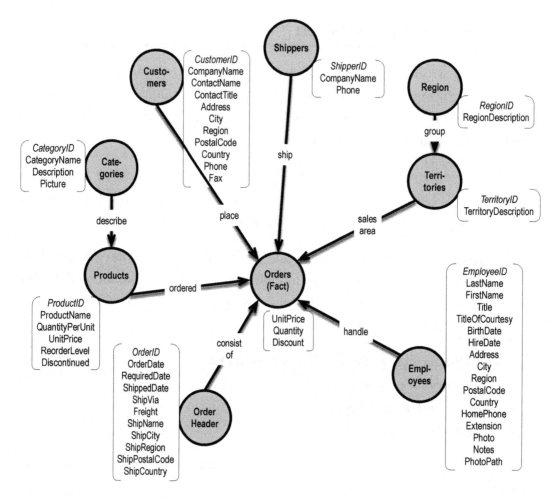

Also notice that there are some explicit hierarchies:

- Categories to products

- Regions to territories.

There are also some implicit denormalized relationships (dependencies) inside the entity types in the relational model:

- Various roles of dates with respect to a calendar dimension

- Various roles of geography with respect to a country dimension.

Let us visualize those hidden dependencies:

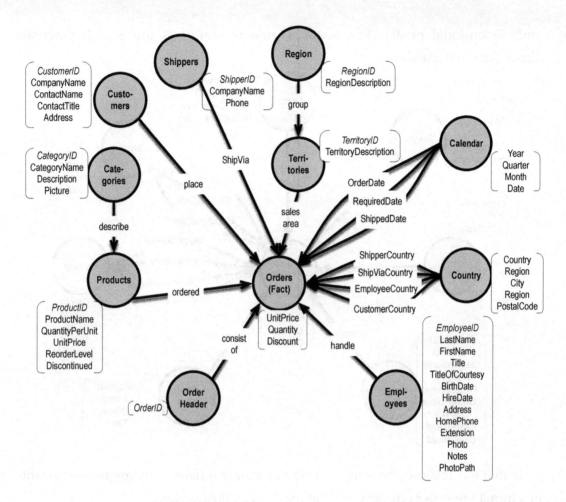

We could also question whether "contact" is an independent entity type. For this exercise, we'll assume that there is a business rule saying that we maintain only one contact per customer.

Also note that the order header has degenerated into an OrderID. We will push that to the fact table, and get rid of the dimension (which will just become a passive property of the orders fact).

Good "Kimballian" star schema design does not accept so-called "snowflake" designs of dimensions, so we will denormalize the hierarchies into flat dimension tables. We'll also skip some operational details (such as phone numbers, photo path, and pictures). Finally, there are some naming issues once we get to the final multidimensional model. The textbook rule is that facts are plural, whereas dimensions are singular.

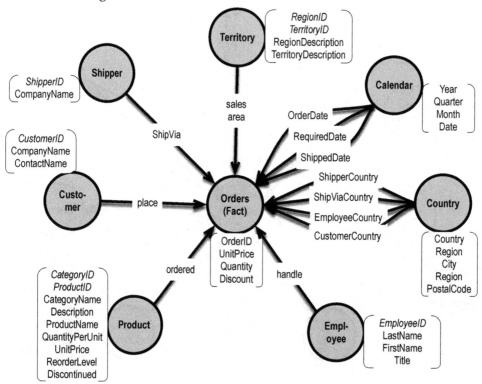

Note that the dates on the employee are not included here. They might be relevant in a human resources context, but not really in an orders context.

Since an important aspect of multidimensional data models is the issue of hierarchies, you might be hesitant to hide the relationships in the territory and product dimensions. I recommend documenting these as concept maps, like this:

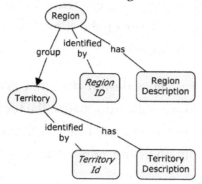

And this:

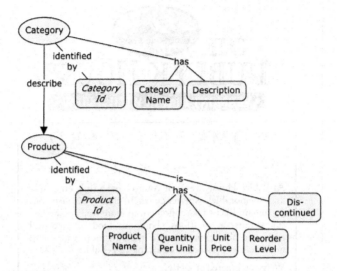

Notice that the "is" dependency between product and discontinued may imply that there is a business event called "product discontinuation" or similar; this event could be a business object type in its own right.

5.3. A Survey Form

In Steve Hoberman's book *Data Modeling for MongoDB* [9] we find a case study based on the transformation of a survey form to a logical data model, and then on to a collection-based model for the document database characteristics of Mongo DB. With Steve's kind permission, the next page contains the survey form.

Apart from the form, the data model that Steve develops must also include the surrounding information that a company conducting a survey would require.

The data model in relational style appears on the following page.

COMMENT CARD

Server _____ Date _____

At Publyk House, we want you to have a truly enjoyable and memorable experience each time you visit our restaurant. Please take a moment to share your comments, suggestions or questions about our food, service and ambiance. Your comments are intended for private use to make your experience as enjoyable as possible.

Were you greeted properly?

POOR   1 ☐   2 ☐   3 ☐   4 ☐   5 ☐   EXCELLENT

How was your server?

POOR   1 ☐   2 ☐   3 ☐   4 ☐   5 ☐   EXCELLENT

How was the atmosphere?

POOR   1 ☐   2 ☐   3 ☐   4 ☐   5 ☐   EXCELLENT

How was the price/value?

POOR   1 ☐   2 ☐   3 ☐   4 ☐   5 ☐   EXCELLENT

What is your favorite menu item & your least favorite?
Why? _____

_____

_____

How did you hear about us? _____

Do you plan on coming back?   ☐ Yes   ☐ No

Would you recommend us to a friend?   ☐ Yes   ☐ No

If you would like to receive promotional e-mails, including new menu items, please write down your email address:

_____

Your comments: _____

_____

_____

_____

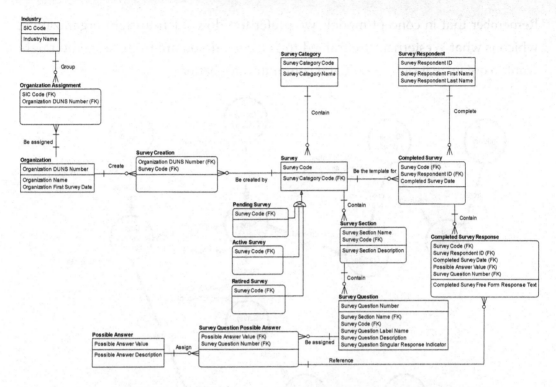

As an overview, the business object type level concept model looks like this:

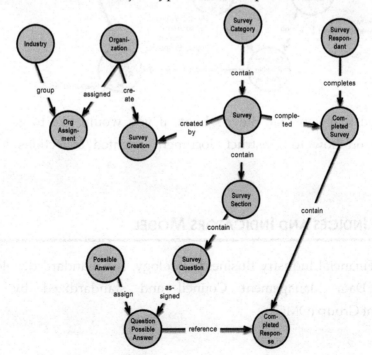

Remember that in concept models we prefer top-down, left-to-right organization, which is what Westerners are trained to perceive. If you are from Asia, you might want to organize it right-to-left, if it communicates better.

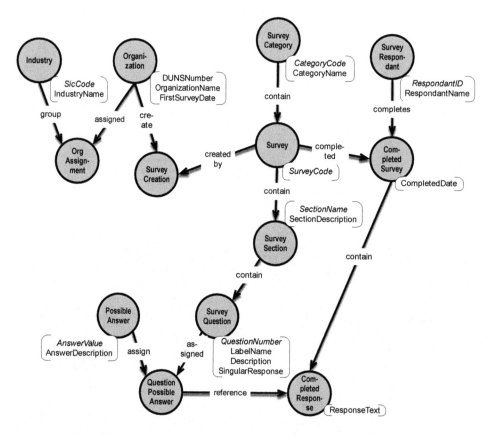

I recommend that you read Steve's book, if you would like to get an in-depth explanation on how to construct document oriented collections for this data model.

5.4. FIBO INDICES AND INDICATORS MODEL

The FIBO, Financial Industry Business Ontology, is a standard developed by the Enterprise Data Management Council and standardized by the Object Management Group (OMG).

It is an evolving standard that aspires to cover all of the financial industry; it is intended to be used in data interchange between industry parties and with regulators. It has a section containing metadata for indices and indicators, such as benchmark indices and other rates as well as national economic indicators. This section is what we'll take a stab at modeling.

The reference document is: EDMC- Financial Industry Business Ontology (FIBO), Indices and Indicators, Version 1.0 - Beta 2 Release Date: May 2015, dtc/15-05-11, Beta 2, PDF http://bit.ly/29PoJBh.

The rates and indicators span the following concepts (simplified for pedagogical reasons):

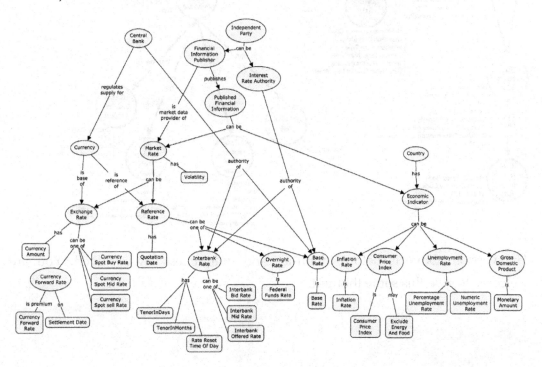

Here the concepts and relationships are transformed into a solution data model design:

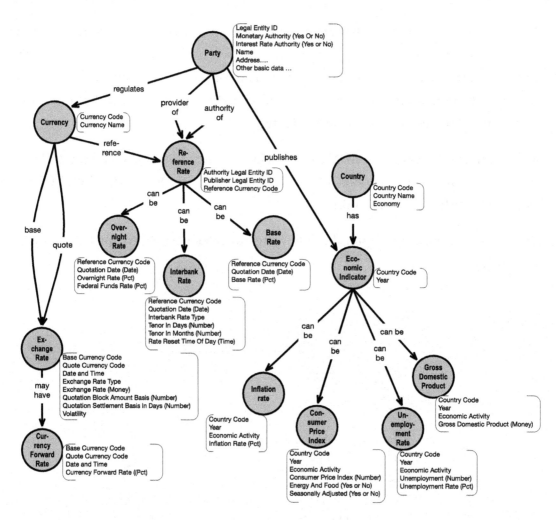

The version above is before identities and uniqueness are resolved. You are welcome to give this some thought.

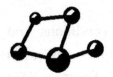

Chapter 6
Before Your Expedition Begins

6.1. ESSENTIAL SKILLS AND INSIGHTS FOR YOUR "EXPEDITIONS"

Data modeling is a journey into lands of the unknown. A journey of exploration, discovery, and mapping. Every capable discoverer knows that there are certain things you must keep with you at all times. Here are my best bets on concepts you should keep in your "mental backpack," wherever your modeling efforts take you.

The priorities are:

1) Structure
2) Content.

Remember that structure is top priority, but the combination of structure and content is what meaning is made of.

Today, the demand for a 3-layered modeling approach is more important than ever before. When relational modeling was dominant, everything melted into a pot of "table soup," which was called a variety of things such as entity-relationship, conceptual, logical and more. This is no longer an option, since many projects are now being based on physical models without tables.

The distinction between the business layer (i.e. concept models) and the solution layer is that the business layer is a map of reality, whereas the solution layer is a design artifact effectively scoping a particular IT solution (probably containing a number of generalizations and/or other design decisions).

One of the ongoing discussions is that of how to draw a line in the sand between data models and business rules. First of all, business rules "fit into" the concept and data models. From an overall perspective, all those "if...then...else..." rules contain business concepts in the formulations of both the conditions and consequences. Having said that, there is still the issue of whether any given specification is at the data model level or at the business rule level. The transitions can be quite subtle and difficult to notice as you go. My recommendation is:

If a specification contains actual data in the text, then it is a business rule. For example, "...greater than five business days..." is a rule, not a part of the data model. A 3-layer data model architecture is the way to go, not least in NoSQL:

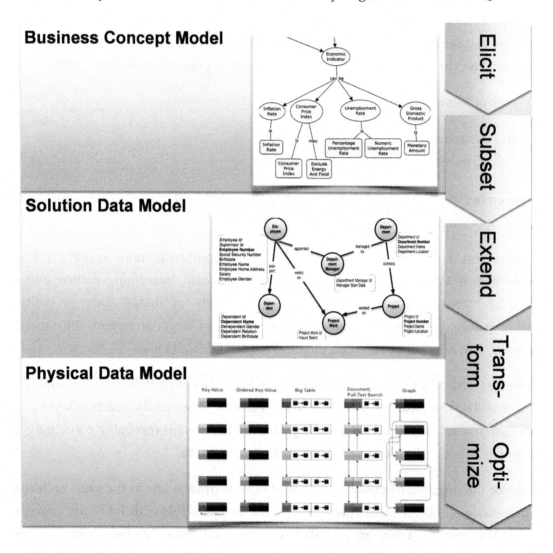

Tables are in the wrong place, if they participate in data models. They are basically external views (in the ANSI-SPARC terminology), designed to represent data in a user interface (e.g. a screen, a form, a grid). Such applications are where tables excel, just look at Excel. Using tables in physical representation is a possibility, but just one among many (like aggregates, key-values and graphs).

The purpose of all this effort is to create business value. Put that idea on top in your backpack! This is ultimately why data modeling is important. Since businesses are run by humans, they are somewhat "fluffy." This is why it's critical to understand and apply cognitive and psychological findings. Learning is a big part of data modeling; psychologists have been busy for over 50 years. Being "fluffy" also means that issues such as uniqueness and identity can have exceptions in the real world. So be flexible!

The "I" in IT stands for information, and that is our business. Getting information across is the essence of communication. We must be proficient in getting our structure and content inside people's heads. We build maps of the information landscape and, being the discoverers, we help our peers to navigate a complex context.

When you look back at what happened within database and data modeling history, it is an astounding hindsight that the discipline is still so new! The pioneers spent a lot of time and effort on learning to stand up and stand still, just like Bambi on ice. I have never seen a specification of the non-functional requirements of a data modeling solution. That is why I included it in this book.

Pointers are all right, as long as they are not physically bound. Graph databases deserve more credit.

Properties of a business type are all at the same "location in the conceptual space," by definition. This indicates that the business object types are the "landmarks" of the data model, resembling an "information landscape."

Chen did it right with his entity-attribute-relationship models. It is a shame that these models never grew into maturity. Much effort has been spent on understanding normalization and on taking it into eight layers of "normal forms." Seems to me that a number of issues are being put into the normalization melting pot. It remains unclear that if normalization is the answer, what was the question, again? The key question(s) in data modeling should be concerned with exploring and mapping structure, meaning, identity and uniqueness.

Cognitive computing (including semantics and machine learning) is rapidly evolving, within metadata capture and automated data modeling. This could change the "Analyze" phase of the closed loop:

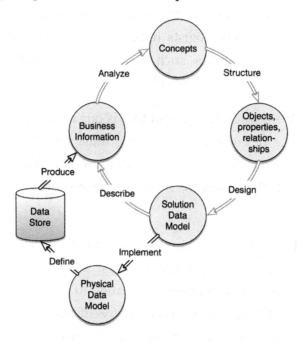

Automated discovery of relationships is the "next big thing" in data modeling, and graphs are excellent for visualizing relationships.

Never forget that one size does not fit all. However, property graphs are the most independent representations that can span the whole spectrum of physical paradigms on the table today—with or without tables. Data today is highly dimensional; in the context of data modeling, this means that it is full of relationships. That is where graphs excel.

Especially in concept mapping, the data modeler should have a degree of artistic freedom to find his or her own style. The important thing is that the messages are delivered to the readers, as effortlessly and reliably as can be. Play around with layout, styles, colors, fonts, images, and the lot. The goal is to fascinate and then mesmerize you audience.

Here I have played around a little with gradient fillings and shadows to get a more modern style:

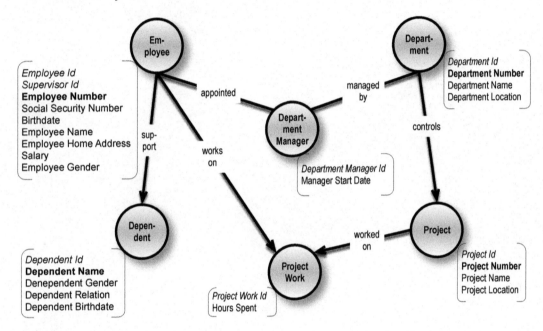

Have fun!

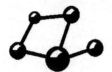

Literature

[1] Date, C.J.: A Guide to the SQL Standard, Addison-Wesley, 1987.

[2] Date, C.J.: An Introduction to Database Systems, Volume I, Fourth Edition, AddisonWesley, 1986.

[3] Date, C.J.: Database Design and Relational Theory, Normal Forms and All That Jazz, 2012 O'Reily.

[4] Devlin, B.: Business unIntelligence, Insight and Innovation beyond Analytics and Big Data, Technics Publications, 2013.

[5] Frisendal, T.: Design Thinking Business Analysis - Business Concept Mapping Applied, Thomas Frisendal, © Springer, 2012.

[6] Gärdenfors, P.: The Geometry of Meaning, Semantics based on Conceptual Spaces, 2014 MIT Press.

[7] Halpin, T., Morgan, T.: Information Modeling and Relational Databases, Morgan Kaufmann, 2008.

[8] Hay, D.C.: Data Model Patterns, A Metadata Map, Morgan Kaufmann, 2006, © David Hay.

[9] Hoberman, S.: Data Modeling for MongoDB, Building Well-Designed and Supportable MongoDB Databases, Technics Publications, 2014.

[10] Katsov, I.: NoSQL Data Modeling Techniques, Highly Scalable Blog, March, 2012.

[11] Moon, B., Hoffman, R.R. Novak, J., Canas, A.: Applied Concept Mapping: Capturing, Analyzing, and Organizing Knowledge, CRC Press, 2011.

[12] Sadalage, P.J, Fowler, M.: NoSQL Distilled: A Brief Guide to the Emerging World of Polyglot Persistence, Addison-Wesley Professional; 1 edition, August 18, 2012.

For further reference on IDMS, see this site: http://bit.ly/2ax32GY, or this site: http://bit.ly/29QIA2n.

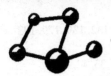

Index

3-Schema Architecture, 17, 30

Abstraction, 175, 177

aggregates, 12, 123, 132, 133, 134, 187, 191, 219

ANSI-SPARK, 17, 30, 219

BABOK, 70, 129

Big Data, 4, 5, 11, 12, 15, 17, 58, 59, 78, 87, 98, 223

Business Glossary, 97

business objects, 68, 91, 112, 124, 127, 128, 130, 131, 135, 136, 152, 158, 159, 175, 176, 198

business rules, 3, 51, 52, 53, 69, 125, 129, 135, 156, 183, 217

cardinality, 154, 155

Charles M. Bachman, 26

Chris Date, 33, 34, 35, 37, 100, 108, 112

CmapTools, 6, 71, 89

Cognition, 6, 60, 61, 71

cognitive computing, 48, 77, 78

Cognitive psychology, 60

collections, 123, 133, 134, 193, 194, 214

Concept extraction, 97

concept map, 66, 67, 69, 70, 74, 89, 92, 103, 109, 147, 148, 152, 153, 157, 159, 163, 170

Concept mapping, 64

Concept Model, 122, 123, 125, 139

concepts, 10, 42, 46, 47, 48, 51, 52, 65, 66, 68, 69, 70, 76, 80, 89, 90, 91, 96, 97, 113, 124, 127, 128, 135, 136, 153, 158, 159, 164, 167, 168, 175, 176, 180, 181, 197, 199, 215, 218

Conceptual modeling, 64, 84, 102

Conceptual Spaces, 71, 73, 223

Cullinane, 17

Cullinet, 39

data modeling processes, 11

data profiling, 94, 95, 96, 98

Data Structure Diagram, 7, 17, 27

data types, 104, 125, 135, 159, 171

DB2, 17, 19, 26, 39

DBOMP, 17, 21, 22, 23

denormalization, 84, 123, 134, 187, 189, 190, 191, 192, 193, 201

denormalized, 41, 133, 189, 199, 202, 205, 207

design, 35, 37, 53, 71, 84, 88, 99, 122, 123, 127, 136, 144, 146, 150, 162, 163, 175, 187, 192, 193, 208, 215, 217

directed graphs, 43, 49, 69, 80, 81, 105, 130, 136, 149

document stores, 187, 193

E. F. (Ted) Codd, 55

elicitation, 87, 122, 124, 135

entity extraction, 96

Entity-Relationship, 19, 29, 31, 50, 64, 102

foreign keys, 33, 43, 53, 104, 110, 160, 162, 168, 182

Foreign keys, 201

Functional dependencies, 93, 99

functional dependency graph, 99

Generalization, 90, 177

Google Knowledge Graph, 62

graph database, 18, 44, 45, 101, 181, 184, 185

Hierarchical data structures, 38

hierarchies, 25, 157, 158, 175, 176, 184, 187, 189, 190, 193, 199, 207, 208, 209

Identity, 124, 150, 160, 161, 162, 167

IDMS, 17, 24, 27, 28, 39, 40

IHMC, 6, 71

IMS, 17, 24, 26, 28, 39, 40

Informix, 39

Key/Value, 45, 187

knowledge graph, 74, 77, 97

Linkurious, 120

logical data model, 15, 84, 85, 210

Machine learning, 78

Many-to-many relationships, 91, 176

Michael Stonebraker, 56

multidimensional, 18, 61, 63, 151, 182, 187, 202, 205, 206, 209

Neo4J, 116

nested object types, 176, 180

Network data structures, 38

NIAM, 149

normal form, 36, 100, 142, 143, 144, 145, 146

normalization, 4, 9, 37, 38, 57, 99, 100, 101, 128, 139, 140, 146, 150, 160, 161, 220

NoSQL, 5, 6, 11, 17, 19, 24, 50, 58, 59, 60, 84, 132, 159, 187, 223

Object Orientation, 41

Object-Role-Modeling, 51

OMG, 6, 52, 65, 70, 214

One-to-many relationships, 91

One-to-one relationships, 91, 175

optionality, 154, 156

Oracle, 17, 19, 39, 105, 204

ORM, 47, 50, 51, 53, 129, 149

pattern, 153, 164, 193

Peter Chen, 17, 30, 50, 163

physical data model, 84

pointers, 21, 22, 26, 28, 33, 79, 81, 150

Primary key, 53

properties, 43, 45, 46, 49, 67, 68, 73, 76, 89, 91, 106, 113, 125, 127, 128, 131, 135, 136, 147, 152, 154, 159, 161, 164, 173, 177, 179, 180, 181, 182, 190, 195, 197, 205

property graph, 3, 18, 44, 49, 50, 112, 126, 130, 131, 133, 136, 170, 181, 182, 184, 197, 200, 204

property graph data model, 50, 130, 136

query optimizer, 33

RDF, 18, 46, 47, 48, 73, 76, 108, 133, 178, 187, 194, 195, 196, 197

redundancy, 35, 36, 100, 132, 139, 179, 193

Relational Data Model, 9

Relational Model, 17, 32, 35, 44, 203

Relationship Discovery, 97

relevance, 12, 13, 15

relvar, 33, 34, 36, 37, 161

repeating groups, 142, 143, 176, 191

SBVR, 6, 47, 52, 65, 70, 129

semantic, 42, 45, 46, 47, 51, 53, 62, 73, 75, 76, 77, 97, 131, 178, 187, 194, 197

Semantic Web, 46, 73, 75, 76, 108, 197

solution data model, 85, 89, 122, 126, 129, 132, 133, 134, 137, 152, 153, 154, 159, 162, 179, 180, 186, 189, 190, 193, 195, 197, 198, 200, 215

spatial, 61, 63, 80

specialization, 177

SQL, 3, 6, 9, 16, 18, 19, 23, 32, 33, 39, 40, 44, 50, 57, 99, 105, 128, 133, 150, 151, 154, 156, 157, 181, 185, 187, 189, 199, 200, 201, 203, 204, 223

subtypes, 177, 178, 179

surrogate key, 53, 54, 168, 170

terminology, 9, 10, 53, 85, 90, 123, 124, 125, 126, 134, 135, 153, 161, 176, 177, 219

Terry Halpin, 53

Text mining, 96

UML, 18, 19, 41, 47, 52, 53, 61, 64, 76, 102, 107, 129

uniqueness, 54, 124, 127, 132, 136, 150, 151, 160, 161, 162, 166, 167, 168, 169, 189, 216, 219

Unknown, 157

versioning, 174, 175, 187

Visualization, 12, 81, 98, 99, 102, 107

V-words, 12

W3C, 18, 46, 75, 197

XML, 18, 46, 73, 113, 196

Lightning Source UK Ltd.
Milton Keynes UK
UKOW05f0243150218
317905UK00005BB/194/P